What people are saying about …

Make Love, Make War

"My wife Stasi and I have loved Brian's music for years. We use it at our retreats! We love the heart of the man behind this book—his understanding of the heart of God, and how vital real, intimate worship is to the battle we all find ourselves in."

John & Stasi Eldredge, Ransomed Heart Ministries

"A delicious feast of 'big song' stories, gripping Old Testament narratives, and profound personal anecdotes. As if pulling the curtain back, Brian weaves together a powerful collection of ideas that take us into the inner workings of the songwriting process while pointing all believers toward a healthy and inspiring view of what the church can be when we are willing to embrace our purpose. Brian is a veteran voice crying in the wilderness, calling the church forward to authentic, transformational worship."

Paul Baloche, songwriter, author, pastor

"In *Make Love, Make War,* Brian Doerksen speaks often of the Trinity, the three-in-one God. The root must run deep, for Brian's book is marked by its own three-in-oneness: it's an anthology of backstories to some of the greatest worship songs of our generation, a compendium of trade secrets for seasoned or aspiring songsmiths, and a meditation, both pastoral and scholarly, on the character of God, all unified by the obvious love Brian has for God and His bride. I wholeheartedly recommend this book. It will inspire and instruct all who write (or want to write) songs for the church, and it will deepen and refresh all who sing them."

Mark Buchanan, author of *The Rest of God*

"This book grounds the reader in what matters most as we steward the staggering privilege of calling others into worship. I love the honesty of Brian's stories, the wisdom of his perspective and experience, and the way all of it points us toward a deeper love for God and the church. What a gift these words are for the creation of an ever-more-radiant bride of Christ."

Nancy Beach, champion for the arts at Willow Creek Association, teaching pastor at Willow Creek Community Church

"We all have people that we look up to, who inspire and challenge us. For me Brian is one such person. Here is a great book that captures his passion, wisdom, and deep integrity. Anyone excited about growing as a worship leader, songwriter, or worshipper should read this."

Tim Hughes, music artist, songwriter, and worship director at Holy Trinity Brompton

"Here is a modern psalmist at work, revealing the story behind the memorable melodies and engaging lyrics of his pioneering worship songs. Real and personal, it is yet the preeminent Story not only of the Father's love, but also, His fierce determination to deliver His children from destruction into destiny."

Gordon Dalbey, author of *Healing the Masculine Soul* and *No Small Snakes: A Journey into Spiritual Warfare*

"Lucidly written and beautifully practical, *Make Love, Make War* gives us a fresh opportunity to engage with the story behind so many of the songs we sing today, and embrace all over again the life contained within them."

Kathryn Scott, worship leader and songwriter of "Hungry," "At the Foot of the Cross," and "I Belong"

"Brian has exquisitely captured the pure passion of worship—our intimacy with God! Not only has he shared the joy and challenge of his 'real-life' experience, but we are blessed recipients of wisdom through his outstanding songwriter tips. Without a doubt, *Make Love, Make War* is a must read for everyone in worship ministry."

Howard Rachinski, president and CEO, Christian Copyright Licensing International

"I had the privilege of experiencing the powerful impact of many of Brian's songs as they were first introduced. With the same masterful touch that Brian used to craft these invitations to worship, he has called forth wisdom and wonder and brought these songs to life in me again. As inspiring as it is practical, this book doesn't lead us to focus on the songs themselves but on the One who gave them!"

Gary Best, national team leader, Vineyard Churches Canada

"Brian Doerksen has been a great friend and teacher to me. Some of my fondest memories of my time in England are in the Doerksen home, surrounded by the tribe of Doerksen children and having some of my hardest worship questions answered by Brian and Joyce. Brian is obviously a very gifted songwriter. But he is also a patient and honest teacher. I am sure this book will be of help to you, as Brian has been of help to me."

Brenton Brown, songwriter and worship leader

"Brian has done a beautiful job of combining the essence of worship and faith. Deep scriptural truths stand behind the words of every song. As I read *Make Love, Make War* and listened to the music in each chapter, I was moved in the depths of my soul."

Tom Davis, president of Children's HopeChest, and author of *Red Letters* and *Scared*

"This book is a rare gem. Brian is one of the very few songwriters and worship leaders who have a genuine focus on the Father-heart of God. He has been a lone voice and a brave pioneer in this regard, forging genuinely Trinitarian songs on the anvil of his deep and sometimes painful journey with Abba, Father. Brian has never settled for unbiblical sentimentality and superficiality. Every chapter of this book contains practical and profound wisdom. No one interested in Christian worship can afford to be without this study. It is destined to become a classic. I unreservedly recommend this powerful and unique blend of honest storytelling and luminous teaching."

Dr. Mark Stibbe, author and leader of The Fathers House Trust

MAKE LOVE, MAKE WAR
NOW Is the Time to Worship

BRIAN DOERKSEN

David C Cook®
transforming lives together

MAKE LOVE, MAKE WAR
Published by David C. Cook
4050 Lee Vance View
Colorado Springs, CO 80918 U.S.A.

David C. Cook Distribution Canada
55 Woodslee Avenue, Paris, Ontario, Canada N3L 3E5

David C. Cook U.K., Kingsway Communications
Eastbourne, East Sussex BN23 6NT, England

Survivor is an imprint of David C. Cook, Kingsway Communications Ltd.
info@survivor.co.uk

David C. Cook and the graphic circle C logo
are registered trademarks of Cook Communications Ministries.

The Web site addresses recommended throughout this book are offered as a
resource to you. These Web sites are not intended in any way to be or imply an
endorsement on the part of David C. Cook, nor do we vouch for their content.

LCCN 2009928005
ISBN 978-1-4347-6682-3
eISBN 978-1-4347-0043-8

The Team: John Blase, Amy Kiechlin, Sarah Schultz, Jaci
Schneider, Caitlyn York, and Karen Athen
Cover design: Big [Brand Innovation Group, LLC] Creative Team
Cover Photo: iStockphoto, royalty free

Printed in the United States of America
First Edition 2009

1 2 3 4 5 6 7 8 9 10

052909

For all of you worshippers who sing in the midst of suffering and hiddenness ...

You may think you are small, but you are significant in the eyes of God.

You may think you are forgotten—but just like the woman who poured perfume on Jesus' feet, you will be remembered in the halls of heaven, and your reward will be great!

CONTENTS

Acknowledgments		11
Introduction		13
Chapter 1	Come, Now Is the Time to Worship	17
Chapter 2	Holy God	39
Chapter 3	Father, I Want You to Hold Me	65
Chapter 4	Refiner's Fire	87
Chapter 5	Fortress 144	109
Chapter 6	Today (As for Me and My House)	129
Chapter 7	Psalm 13 (How Long O Lord)	143
Chapter 8	Your Faithfulness	165
Chapter 9	Hallelujah (Your Love Is Amazing)	177
Chapter 10	It's Time for the Reign of God	195
Chapter 11	With All My Affection	215
Chapter 12	Song for the Bride (Isaiah 30:15)	233

This book exists because several people encouraged me and believed that I had the words in me:

Don Pape—you saw something, and you made the call that got it rolling. Thanks for believing in me and for your encouragement that I could do something that I hadn't done before.

Pam Dyck and the women in my prayer shield—on a trip to Colorado Springs, the group of you were praying for me (**Pam, Valerie Ensor, Rebecca van Noppen, and Diane Friesen**), and you saw a picture of me writing a book. If it wasn't for your confirmation, prayers, and encouragement, I'm not sure this book would exist.

John Blase—what a gift and gifted writer you are! Your editing input has helped me express my heart. Thank you for all the gentle encouragement in the journey.

Gary Best—you were the first pastor in the church that saw some of my potential even though I was so young and full of young man stuff. You watched me over the years get some of the stuffing knocked out of me, and you still believed in me. I just want you to know that I'm still grateful for your faith in me.

Carol Wimber, Jeremy Cook, and all at Vineyard Music—for the early years of sharing my intimate worship songs with the church.

Hans Groeneveld, John Coleman, Chris Springer, and my Integrity family—thanks for believing that I have something to say to the church as a worship songwriter and for doing everything you can to get the songs out there.

Karin Esau—your prophetic insight and help with my administration and ministry requests have helped keep me alive these past years. Thanks for taking care of so many things so I can take care of what God has called me to do.

Dean and Janine Richmond, Dave and Dee Hensman, Irv and Karin Esau—my friends and team of pastors at the Bridge in Abbotsford, British Columbia. What amazing joy it is to serve with you. Thank you for blessing and releasing me to serve the broader church through projects like this.

Joyce—you are my biggest support and best friend. You help me discern like no other my true calling, and you keep me grounded in ways that are full of life! Thanks for supporting me through every stage of writing this book.

INTRODUCTION

The picture was surprising and striking.

Puzzling, even.

It wasn't the kind of picture one would expect to see in the middle of worship on the Lord's Day at your local church.

This picture, like an open vision, looked like one of the memorable scenes from the hippie movement—a number of bedraggled-looking young people holding up a sign.

The sign read "MAKE LOVE, NOT WAR."

As I continued looking, something strange started happening. One of the words began to change before my eyes. Now the sign read "MAKE LOVE, MAKE WAR." And as soon as that one word changed, I sensed the presence of God; He was now holding the sign.

Four words shaped into a clarion call, a prophetic sign to brave and free worshippers everywhere.

Could that be true?

Could God possibly be saying something that provocative?

I believe we know that love and war are at the heart of everything inside us and everything going on all around us. We know that we are in the middle of an ancient war. We sense that there is nothing that Satan hates more than the worship of YHWH by those who are faithful to the Lamb. When we worship, we do what Satan abandoned long ago—and the Enemy does everything he can to stop us from worshipping, because when we worship, he remembers. He spends more than a little energy convincing us that there really is no war going on and that the sum total of our life's calling is to be nice.

He is greatly relieved when we drop our swords and retreat from the battle.

He laughs when we lose heart and fall away from loving God.

God *is* saying something provocative—but not something that causes us to fall. He's provoking us to rise up!

What we see on the sign reveals what we believe about God and His character.

If the sign read "MAKE WAR, NOT LOVE," what would that tell us?

The God who is revealed in the Scriptures would not be holding that sign! Not only do we need love, but we also need to realize that love has to come first—and it needs to be the kind of love that Jesus came to reveal.

It may be easy for us to smugly look back on the hippie era and say, "They focused on the wrong kind of love … and the wrong war." But we should realize that our generation has done the same!

That's why I believe that God is holding up the sign I saw to our generation.

God is calling us to love, and He is calling us to battle. And the war to which God calls us is always waged for the sake of love!

There are many ways to express love and to participate in the battle. It's the way we live our lives; it's the way we serve, defend, and protect. One of the ways I make love and war is through music.

I had no idea that I would become a songwriter. I just started walking with God, and the songs followed. Some of the songs were honest and intimate expressions of love. Other songs were desperate cries in the middle of the battle.

And that's one of the amazing things about songs in worship. They powerfully focus our expressions of love and war. Sometimes a song is a love song, a way of expressing our devotion to the One who redeemed us. Love songs are going to fill eternity as we journey deeper and deeper into intimacy with our God. Other songs awaken and strengthen us for the battle—and those songs are sometimes sung and played with such intensity that even our enemies hear them and fear! I resonate with the true story recorded in 2 Chronicles 20. The worshippers went ahead of the soldiers, and as they worshipped, their enemies' hearts melted with fear. That kind of worship is still happening today. That's the kind of worship I want to spend my life on: worship that is passionate, intimate, and full of the presence of God!

I want to spend my life in worship as an act of love and war.

I hope and pray that the stories behind these songs and the truths they sing will awaken your heart to "MAKE LOVE, MAKE WAR" for the glory of God!

In the Father's love,
Brian Doerksen
The Shining Rose—Abbotsford, British Columbia, Canada

Come, Now Is the Time to Worship

Come, now is the time to worship
Come, now is the time to give your heart
Come, just as you are to worship
Come, just as you are before your God
Come

One day every tongue will confess
You are God
One day every knee will bow
Still the greatest treasure remains for those
Who gladly choose You now

Willingly we choose to surrender our lives
Willingly our knees will bow
With all our heart, soul, mind, and strength
We gladly choose you now[1]

CHAPTER 1

Come, Now Is the Time to Worship

From the moment I "heard" the beginning of this song floating through the air early on a September morning in London, England, I knew something special was happening.[2]

In the mid-1990s I had become somewhat disillusioned with worship music and the ministry connected with it. I grew tired of the striving, weary of artists jumping on the worship bandwagon just because worship music projects were selling more units. There was also my own shallowness as I compared myself with some of those artists. Looking back, I can see that I was passing through a patch of wilderness; God desired to break me in different ways so He could use me in new ways.

In the previous five years, I had experienced some successes with songs and recording projects (all of which were a surprise) and some failures, too (not a huge surprise but still discouraging!). I had also spent a good portion of those years pursuing a dream to communicate the Father-heart of God through music and story in a musical called *Father's House*. The project collapsed for several reasons at the end of 1996.[3] In the process I reached a low point, a point where I was not even sure I believed in God anymore. Or maybe I believed in God but had decided He simply wound up the universe and for the most part abandoned us to sort ourselves out. Rather than finding a figurative corner to "suck my thumb" and feel sorry for myself after the musical collapsed, I decided to try to find a place in the church where I could serve someone else's vision for a few seasons, rather than try to keep my own visions alive. And so God, in His great compassion for my family and my wife, Joyce, moved us to England.

I was given two jobs upon arrival. The first was as the worship pastor at the South West London Vineyard under the leadership of John and Eleanor Mumford. The second one involved training songwriters and worship leaders in the Vineyard movement throughout England, Scotland, and Ireland. There were about seventy-five Vineyard churches in the United Kingdom and Ireland at that time.

It was challenging to do a good job leading worship when so much of my heart was still ravaged by confusion and disappointment. But I had served long enough in the church to know how to effectively gather up people in the presence of God through intimate worship, and so I just got on with it, believing that eventually my feelings and the restoration of my heart would follow. I do remember a few times when I gulped rather deeply before getting up to lead worship, wondering if God might strike me down for leading in public, when privately I was having doubts about His very existence—or at the least, doubts about His goodness and whether He was actively intervening on behalf of His children. Yet where else could I turn? I knew enough about the other major philosophies and religions to know that nothing else really made sense of life and death, nor satisfied my heart and awakened my spirit.

Most mornings I would get up before the kids to go for a brisk walk. It was some light daily exercise and a chance to clear my mind before the day began. And it was also time to pray, to sing, and to speak out Scriptures. It was on one of these walks that I heard it. The idea floated through the air, and in that moment my life changed again. I tuned into what felt like the "frequency of worship"—that realm where God is completely real—and I immediately sensed the presence of God in a way that I had not for some time. I intuitively knew I was tuning into God's invitation, the invitation that goes out "day after day," as it says in Psalm 19:

> The heavens declare the glory of God; the skies proclaim the work of his hands. Day after day they pour forth speech; night after night they display knowledge. There is no speech or language where their voice is not heard. Their voice goes out into all the earth, their words to the ends of the world. (vv. 1–4)

The call to worship is unending. Its sound reverberates in every language and culture … and I was just hearing a little part of it in English in England's capital city on that September morning. It is so amazing how big a little fragment of "God inspiration" can be!

Once the idea came, I kept singing it over and over so I wouldn't lose it. (I have heard stories of songwriters who get a brilliant idea but lose it because they don't sing it enough to imprint it or write it down or record it some way.) When I got home, I raced upstairs to the piano in the top loft of the house, and I started playing the idea over and over. I took a mental picture of playing the melody on the piano and jotted down some notes and phrases that popped into my head. In the few minutes before I left for my favorite daily job of walking my kids to school, I managed to document the basic idea of the first section of the song. I don't remember the details of that morning walk with the kids. Usually I drive them crazy by singing silly songs—whatever I see sparks a song, and I love embarrassing them by being silly. It's part of the dad job description. However, I expect that morning there were no silly songs ... just the repetition of this God-breathed melody.

Over the rest of the week, I continued to sing the song—morning, afternoon, and evening. Writing a song feels more like birthing, and it invades every waking thought.

If you had told me that this song would travel the globe, get translated into numerous languages, and be recorded by dozens of artists, I probably would have chuckled in disbelief ... but just maybe I would have said, "Yes, that's going to happen." I sensed that God was designing and building something special, and by His grace, He was letting me in on the ground floor.

About a week later I felt like the song was basically finished. That's pretty quick for me—sometimes I take months with songs as they go through multiple drafts. The next Sunday I tried the song out at our home church: the SW London Vineyard.[4]

The song connected right away. In fact it seemed only a few weeks later that I heard that the song was already being used in South Africa. Often people interested in or connected to the Vineyard Movement would visit our church as they passed through London, sometimes taking songs with them as they headed home to other places. I was amazed to hear that the song had already traveled to the other side of the world. I had heard stories of other songs that spread that quickly, but to have it happen to a song I had written seemed crazy!

But even crazier is this: I wrote this song at one of the lowest points of my life—the point where I had failed in a big way with a project publicly, the point when private doubts raged about this whole "Christian ministry" and serving God thing. But that explains some of the lyric choices I made.

I think if someone in a season of success had received the same melodic idea and opening line, the song may have turned into something like this:

> Come, now is the time to worship
> Come, now is the time to give Him praise
> Come, bring Him your best and worship
> Come, give Him your all in glorious praise
> Come

Had this song been written by someone who was flying high, the focus may have been more on the good that we could do for God—but I was feeling broken. I needed to know that I could come and worship God just the way I was and that He would receive me even though my life was not all together. I needed to know that worship was about our heart, not our accomplishments. And so I wrote lines like "give your heart" and "just as you are before your God" because those were the things that I needed to reaffirm. I needed to know that those lines were true. That's what you are constantly doing as a songwriter—stepping back from what you have written and asking yourself, "Are these lines true? Do I need to say that in this season to God?"

Would you like to know a songwriter secret?

We basically write the songs that we need to sing. God by His mercy sometimes enables them to become songs for other people too, but we are writing the things that we really need to say to stay sane and alive! And I think that's a good thing. That's why I challenge worship songwriters to stop trying to write songs that the church around the world will sing and instead try to write a song that they have the courage to sing in their private time with God.

So I wrote the first section of the song as an urgent invitation from God. The key elements were *come, now, time, heart,* and *just as you are.* The second section of the song declares the contrast between the "one day" that is coming and this amazing treasure we receive when we choose to worship God: the treasure of relationship with God.

Think about it this way: Worship is reality.

Being aware of God, focused on Him and in relationship with Him, is ultimate reality. Worship brings that reality into focus. One day reality will be forced on everyone. All people will have to accept the truth that God exists and that He is their Creator and Judge. The tragedy is that He also longed to be their Savior, Father, and Bridegroom.

I have received a few letters over the years from people who have accused me of being a universalist. One man really hoped I was, and he thought he found evidence in this song! A couple of other worship leaders said they wouldn't use the song unless they could change the words. The line they were wrestling with was "still the greatest treasure remains for those who gladly choose You now." Some believed that because I said "greatest treasure," I was suggesting there was a lesser treasure awaiting everyone else—hence Brian Doerksen, the closet universalist.[5]

The greatest treasure I am referring to is the treasure and pleasure of worship: a living, loving relationship with God. I had no intention of implying that those who reject God will get the treasure of eternal life as well. After a few years of answering this question, I am beginning to see how someone could stretch my words to head in that direction; it just never entered my mind, nor did it enter the minds of the theologians I tested the song lyrics with before it was published.

This is one of the challenges of writing for worship: We want to be theologically accurate, but we only have a few phrases to express an idea. Preachers and authors can take one concept and talk or write about it for quite a while! Songwriters take a large amount of material and reduce it to a few phrases that one can remember, forming it into poetic and artistic phrases that sing. If we wanted to fully explain each concept with fifteen verses, the song wouldn't make it very far.[6]

What I was trying to say was that one day all people will be forced to "worship" God with their bodies by bowing their knees, but some are missing this greatest treasure: the experience of worshipping God willingly in the here and now, knowing and loving God and being loved by Him. Instead of living for God, some spend their days seeking earthly treasure, treasure that will be revealed as worthless on that "one day." God remains the only treasure that will always be worthy of our pursuit and devotion!

It seems that the "theological concerns" I received were really about who is going to get into heaven and how that is all going to work. I'm not sure any of us can presume to know those answers.

I can tell you this: Having special-needs sons who cannot communicate verbally has tested me on this point because they can't pray the traditional sinner's prayer. What if the deeper heart questions that God longs for us to ask are "How can I get more heaven into me?" and "How can we get more heaven into us as the community of God?" God alone will be the judge of who enters His presence. And He will be more holy than we could ever imagine … and more merciful! So I'm leaving those matters in His hands. He knows our hearts. He will not force us to choose Him. He invites us to choose Him, and our response to His invitation to "Come" makes all the difference in this life and the next!

Several months after I wrote the song, we started planning the first of two recordings I would produce while living in England in the late 1990s. The first one became known as *Winds of Worship— Live from London* with an alternate title of *Come, Now Is the Time,* and the second one was *Hungry,* which went on to sell over 400,000 copies. The first recording took place on February 22, 1998. It was a Sunday evening, and we were in the Elliot High School auditorium, which was jam-packed with people. It was as if people sensed something special was about to happen. Eleanor Mumford spoke about the treasure of worship before we started the first song, and she encouraged us to worship by singing to the Lord a new song with our whole heart![7]

As we started the song, I sensed God whispering to me, "This is one of the main reasons I brought you across the Atlantic—to encourage and awaken the call to worship in England and Europe in this season." And the entire evening was bathed in the presence of God and charged with an energy and urgency that came from God stirring our hearts. I continued to sense that energy and urgency through the long days of postproduction—and we needed plenty of energy as we only had one week to mix the project, with some days at the studio starting at 9:00 a.m. and not finishing until 4:00 a.m.

That sense of urgency was there because of the urgency to worship. *Now is the time* means just that. Now is the time to choose God, to choose to love and follow Him. We don't know how much time we have left, but we do have today. We have this moment to respond to God's invitation.

This urgency speaks of reordering our priorities. It's time to return to this truth:

> Worship is first …
>> always has been
>> always will be.

It's the way we were made; it's what we were created for!

Worship is the highest privilege and pleasure in the kingdom of God. It is the response of our lives to the greatest commandment in Scripture: "Love the Lord your God with all your heart and with all your soul and with all your mind and with all your strength" (Mark 12:30).

I wrote this song in London, one of the great cities on earth. But it's filled with people who are passionately serving other gods. These days the most common god is the narcissistic trinity of "me, myself, and I." It's a world of people faithful only to themselves, yet made in the image of God, created to worship YHWH. Some activists have declared that this generation can end extreme poverty with our technology and wealth. What a fantastic goal! There is only one challenge: When you have a world of people who are self-absorbed, serving and worshipping themselves and protecting their own rights at any costs, how can we see poverty ended? The only way to see poverty destroyed is to destroy the idolatry that is its root cause.

That's one of the main reasons why there is such urgency to the call to worship that God is sounding. So much hangs in the balance. Those of us who have been called by God to sound this call often come under intense attack. That's one of the reasons why having a "prayer shield" is so vital. Pam Dyck, who leads my team of intercessors, shared this with me recently: "Satan hates what we do when we worship God, for when we embrace the calling to be 'lead worshippers,' we are doing what Satan abandoned." Many theologians believe that there is evidence in Scripture that Satan was a beautiful angel specifically created to direct the worship around the throne to God, until he desired the worship for himself. Of course, we won't know in this life exactly what happened eons ago when Lucifer fell, but we do know that Satan longs to be worshipped—behind all bondage and every false religion is the "father of lies" craving what belongs to God alone.

And so our calling is to clearly and urgently sound the call to worship God. And what is the core of that calling? Nothing less than our hearts—loving God with all of who we are!

And if worship is first and foremost a matter of the heart, it's not about where we worship or what we look like when we worship. It's not a performance for God. It's a surrender of love to God, just the way we are.

It's time to worship.

The word *time* reminds us that we are in the season of worship that God is releasing on the earth. Some people believe that the modern worship music movement "discovered" worship in the last few decades. I think that's proud and ridiculous! I believe that Jesus inaugurated these days when He arrived a short 2,000 years ago, and even Jesus the Son of Man was building upon the worship of the millennium before Him, which included the Davidic house of worship.

Listen to Jesus' words recorded in John 4:

> A time is coming and has now come when the true worshipers will worship the Father in spirit and truth, for they are the kind of worshipers the Father seeks. God is spirit, and his worshipers must worship in spirit and in truth. (vv. 23–24)

The implications of what Jesus is saying here are huge! "We are changing seasons, and I am bringing clear revelation of the truth so that each of us can become the kind of worshipper the Father is seeking."

A time is coming and has now come—and we are in that time now. A time when we are called to worship. What does it really mean to worship? Does it mean merely getting together on Sundays, singing a few songs, and clapping our hands? And why did Jesus speak some of His most direct and instructive words on worship to an outcast woman? Couldn't Jesus have been more strategic? Shouldn't this conversation have happened in the temple with the high priest, with someone who could teach and influence the nation?

I believe one of the many reasons Jesus spoke to the woman about worship is that He wanted to illustrate the contrast between the truth and faithfulness of who He is and the faithlessness and brokenness of our lives filled with fatherless worship. The shame of the woman at the well was the result of men's utter faithlessness. I wonder if her father abandoned her, through neglect or more optimistically through death. If she had known the love of a good father, why would have she sought out the love of so many unfaithful men? Do women with good fathers throw themselves into the arms of scoundrels? Well, yes, we can all probably think of a couple of examples, but those are the exception.

But Jesus spoke to a woman who is miraculously still seeking truth, though there is evidence that she had started to abandon hope, for "the man you now have is not your husband" (John 4:18).

And so Jesus offered this woman two things. One was living water. She had been drinking from the polluted wells of unfaithfulness, which always made her thirsty again. Jesus offered her a well of pure water, water that would satisfy her spiritual thirst. All romantic relationships are inherently spiritual. We know that we are not complete in ourselves, and so we reach out for another to complete us. But because we as humans are all fallen, the only romance that can fully satisfy our hearts is the divine romance.

The second thing Jesus offered was the opportunity to worship the Father. I wonder if she cringed when she heard the word "Father." It seems crazy to me that in our season of history we seem to shy away from this clear biblical revelation. Just because so many men are scoundrels and bad fathers doesn't mean we should not hold out the truth.

Jesus essentially said to the woman, "People just like you who have experienced the pain and rejection of unfaithfulness can be healed. You can become a daughter again, and this time you will encounter true faithfulness. Trust Me. Everyone who worships experiences My faithfulness."

There is no better way to be healed from the effects of unfaithfulness than to give yourself to God in worship. As we worship, our hearts are healed by the faithfulness of God, because that's who God is. Our God is a faithful God!

At the very core of worship is a call to faithfulness, because faithfulness is what's most important to God. How many times in the Old Testament did God send prophets, calling, "Return to Me, faithless people!" (e.g., Jer. 3:14)? We tend to wander away from God and His heart.

> Prone to wander, Lord, I feel it,
> Prone to leave the God I love.[8]

Worship is returning.

There was and is nothing that breaks God's heart more than faithlessness. Can you imagine what Jesus was feeling for this woman? The Father had revealed to Him that this woman's life was filled with failed marriages and unfaithful living. So Jesus came to show her the path to faithfulness, a chance to break free from fatherless worship to worshipping the Father in spirit and truth.

And if nothing breaks God's heart more than faithlessness, we know that nothing brings God greater joy than faithfulness.

God doesn't want to just hear us sing. God wants to see us live a life of faithfulness. The songs that spring from that kind of life will bring God much joy. If people sing of faithful love with their lips but have hearts that are far from Him and lips that are kissing unfaithful lovers, the song they sing is no longer pleasing to God.

Biblical worship is full of truth—truth about who God is coupled with truth about who we are. These truths are essential for real worship. Sometimes God's people are clear on declaring the truth of God, His actions, and His character. But they will never reveal the truth of their lives and struggles in His presence. This leads us in the direction of an artificial or acting faith, where we are always doing "great" and we only sing songs that are happy and full of thanksgiving … and we think we are really worshipping. Well, sometimes we are really lying! I recently read an interview with one of Hollywood's rising talents, and he confessed that actors basically get paid to lie, to pretend to be someone that they are not. Real worship is saturated with truth!

I love the Psalms and I love King David; he's one of my biggest heroes! I often say, "I want to be like Dave!" For centuries the Psalter, the collection of the 150 psalms, was the hymnbook of God's people. I am not advocating that we only sing psalms on this side of the cross. But the Psalms are still full of truth and comfort for God's people today. And they contain truth about God and truth about us as humans. God is not afraid of our humanity. As we come to worship, let's be truthful about who we really are and how we are really doing. Anything else is not real worship.

Listen to Eugene Peterson's version of Jesus' words to the woman:

> But the time is coming—it has, in fact, come—when what you're called will not matter and where you go to worship will not matter. It's who you are and the way you live that count before God. Your worship must engage your spirit in the pursuit of truth. That's the kind of people the Father is out looking for: those who are simply and honestly themselves before him in their worship. (John 4:23 MSG)[9]

In other words, Jesus was saying, "I am thrilled that you are asking about worship, but you are asking the wrong questions. You're asking about *where,* and I am telling you that the most important aspect of worship is *who*—who God is and who you are!"

This woman lived in a world where, like our world today, what you are called matters—your genealogy and roots, your class, your background, your profession, your age, your sex, your name. Those things matter a lot! But Jesus said that a time is being ushered in when labels will not matter anymore. The full and final fulfillment of His words will not happen in this life among the kingdoms of men. But it will happen in the kingdom of heaven! And it happens here on patches of earth where people invite in God's rule and reign.

So Jesus said that "what [we're] called will not matter." Therefore the names that our parents give us and the labels others slap on us are not as important as who we are in the Father's eyes. I can hardly wait for the day in heaven when we get our new name: "He who has an ear, let him hear what the Spirit says to the churches. To him who overcomes, I will give some of the hidden manna. I will also give him a white stone with a new name written on it, known only to him who receives it" (Rev. 2:17).

I think of this name as unique as any individual—no two people will have the same name. I picture God breathing out a word, and that word will be me, will be my name. Maybe that's how God awakens worship in us to start with. He speaks each of our names, and we respond with worship!

But the labels we wear aren't the only things that are throwing us off the track of real worship. It's our focus on the "where" or place of worship. That means that the denomination or type of church we belong to is not the most important thing. (I'm so grateful we are seeing breakthroughs in this as more and more of God's people are learning to walk together.) Nor is the type of building we worship in of ultimate importance. This is a really big one, and to be fair to the people living early in the first century, this was a big shift that Jesus was introducing!

Our labels and locations are so important to us. And we will do almost anything to defend and protect them, often attacking those not like us. The sin of prejudice is probably the most violent sin on earth.

And so Jesus spoke truth to this woman and to us across the centuries. What counts to God is not our labels or our outside appearance. It's our integrity, our honesty, that matters to God. God wants us to come before Him just as we are—God invites us to come with a genuine naturalness, "simply and honestly [ourselves]" (John 4:23 MSG).

You don't have to change *before* you come to worship. You change *because* you have worshipped.

This is in contrast to Psalm 78: "But then they would flatter him with their mouths, lying to him with their tongues; their hearts were not loyal to him, they were not faithful to his covenant" (vv. 36–37).

When we flatter someone, we are just saying what we think he or she wants to hear so that we get something back. Sounds eerily like some modern worship services doesn't it? We fill the air with our "happy-clappy" songs about how wonderful God is so that we get blessed with good feelings and prosperity.

This is the essence of religion: doing everything we can to reach God and make ourselves presentable to Him. This is approaching worship with the attitude that what I give and what I say are the most important things. It all hinges on our performance as we're constantly trying to put our best foot forward. The phrase "Let's put on our Sunday best" has always left a bad taste in my mouth. When it comes to issues like clothing in worship, I believe that God is most delighted when we come dressed the way we live; if you wear a suit during the week and that's the way you live, then please come to worship wearing a suit! But if you live in casual clothes, come to worship the way you live, in casual clothes, as long as the clothes you wear are modest enough not to cause distraction.

The time for religion is over! The time for hype is over! It's time for worship to be saturated with a spirit of humility and honesty. Hype happens when we take our cues from the advertising and image culture all around us. We are supposed to be different from our culture, yet still attractive and accessible.

What I am trying to say—because I believe this is what Jesus was trying to say to the woman—is that the Father is not looking for performance. When we believe that everything hinges on our performance, we often resort to hype and flattery. That's so religious. We should have no time or heart to play that game!

The Father is looking for worshippers, which means He is looking for people. The Father is looking for sons and daughters who will come just as they are, whether weeping with tears or dancing with joy.

It's time to leave behind our fatherless worship, time to break free from orphan living and thinking that fills our lives with striving, competition, and unfaithfulness. It's time to worship the Father in spirit and truth.

Come, *now* is the time to worship.

SONGWRITING TIPS

Document your inspiration when it comes, for it will not come again! I believe that a song starts as a seed—a clear single idea that contains the "songvision" of the song. It's the "one thing" of your song. Make sure when the inspiration comes, when the seed falls into the soil of your life, you plant it! Write it down, record it, and take a mental picture of playing the melody on the piano. Invest in something that makes documenting the idea really simple.

Repetition is good; actually, it's more than good—it's great! Think of the way "Come, Now Is the Time to Worship" repeats the word *come.* I keep on sounding that simple, clear invitation. If you are working on a song, look for the key word that you can repeat.

Make sure you have a strong melodic hook to build on. This song starts with a very clear, strong melodic hook on the third note of the major scale. A good hook is memorable and easy to sing. (Of course, coming up with a fresh hook is always very difficult and is a gift every time it happens!)

Don't waste time. Come right out of the gate with a strong melody and the key thing you want to say lyrically. It's amazing to me how many times writers think they have all day to noodle around with indistinct melodies to "build momentum." You only have momentum if you have something clear right from the start!

It's okay to be unique, to put your personality stamp on your song. One of my key melodic signatures is found in the way the melody is pushed on the last word of line one: "worship." Both of those notes are pushed; they fall on the "four and" before the downbeat. (Of course, I have heard many churches straighten those out, which removes personality and energy from the melody to my ears.) I love melodies that are pushed. What kind of melodies do you love?

Notes

1. Brian Doerksen, "Come, Now Is the Time to Worship," © 1998 Vineyard Songs (UK/Eire). Used by permission.

2. At the time of writing this, I have only "heard" two songs floating through the air; the first one was "Refiner's Fire" in 1989, and the second was "Come, Now Is the Time" in 1997. Most of songwriting for me involves a labor of love, not simply downloading songs from heaven—though I do believe that all inspiration is a gift from God and that we would have nothing without it!

3. Our experience with *Father's House* is a long story about a faith and ministry venture that did not work out, costing us our house and causing many other heartbreaks!

4. We met at Elliot High School in Putney right beside the river Thames within Greater London.

5. One worship leader wrote me about the song with this theological quandary, and then after reading my explanation and wrestling with it a bit more, wrote me back and said, "I introduced your 'greatest treasure' song to our church last Sunday, and many people told me afterwards that they liked 'that new song.' NO ONE mentioned anything about the lyric I was concerned about. I don't get it.

My band loves it!" Of course just to prove how diverse we all are, others wrote and said that line was their favorite line in the song. Over the years I have come to see that music is very subjective—and when you mix subjective musical tastes with theology, which is also subjective and diverse, it makes for some lively and interesting discussions!

6. Unless you are Gordon Lightfoot writing "The Wreck of the Edmund Fitzgerald"!

7. It's Eleanor Mumford's voice you can hear in the swirl at the beginning of the recording.

8. Robert Robinson and John Wyeth, "Come, Thou Fount of Every Blessing," 1759, 1813.

9. Can you hear how some of this paraphrase of Scripture informed aspects of my song "Come, Now Is the Time to Worship"?

Holy God

Holy … Holy
Holy God
(repeat)

Creating, commanding
Transcendent Adonai

Defending love, destroying sin
The warrior divine

Forgiving, redeeming
From every tribe and tongue

Arising first
The nail-scarred Lamb
Salvation's champion

Romancing, pursuing
Reclaiming to restore

Releasing hearts
Transforming lives
The Lion's mighty roar[1]

CHAPTER 2

Holy God

AD 90[2]

A powerful and paranoid emperor named Domitian ruled Rome. He had a few insecurities, so he required everyone to call him *Dominus et Deus,* which means "Lord and God."[3]

The apostle John was preaching the gospel in Ephesus. It was going well—too well for the paranoid emperor, who didn't like people naming Jesus as Lord. Domitian didn't want them believing that Jesus is God's Son, the only incarnation of God on the earth.

And so Domitian decided that it was time to get rid of the disciple whom Jesus loved. First, he tried to kill John by throwing him into a cauldron of boiling oil—but John suffered no harm. Obviously John's time had not yet come; there were more things that God had for John to do.

And so Domitian banished John, sending him to live in exile on the isle of Patmos.

What Satan and Domitian meant for harm, God used for great good.

I am sure John was frustrated with being cut off from the people in Ephesus he was ministering to. I'm sure they were like family to him. And instead of being with them, he was left to wander on a barren island and survive by scratching out an existence. But in his isolation he was not alone. God was there.

Here is where the character of a person like John shines through. Even though he was completely alone—or under Roman guard—John continued his patterns of prayer and worship. Even though no one but God saw what he did, he continued to worship his resurrected Lord on the Lord's Day. And God poured out to him and through him an incredible gift for us all.

And what a gift! As John was worshipping all alone on the Lord's Day on this barren island, God sent him an open vision of the myriad of worshippers before the throne of God.

And what John saw was almost beyond description.

The creatures and beings were fantastical—one like a lion … one like an ox … one like a man … one like an eagle.

But they weren't a lion or an ox or an eagle.

They had six wings, and they were covered with eyes—even under their wings—which makes me wonder: Why would they need eyes there?!

John was trying to describe the indescribable.

Maybe his spiritual eyes were "blinking" after being blinded by all the flashes of light before the throne. He was groping for words and using whatever came to him, for what he was seeing was beyond words.

John was trying to say the unsayable.

But in the center of an indescribable vision was a word—a word the creatures were saying that seemed to hold it all together:

HOLY

But they didn't say the word just once. It came three times—a trilogy repeated without end.

> *"Holy, holy, holy is the Lord God Almighty, who was, and is, and is to come." (Rev. 4:8)*

The word *holy* may be the most important descriptive word of God in the Scriptures. Everything about who He is emanates from His holiness. It's so central and important that those who are worshipping in His immediate presence don't just say it once or twice … they say it three times!

Theologians have come up with a funky word for this "thrice holy" description of God—they call it the trisagion, from the Greek *tris* (three) and *hagios* (holy). Literally trisagion means "thrice holy." It is pronounced "tree-sah-yon."

This window into heavenly worship before the throne of God doesn't just happen in Revelation—it happens over seven hundred years earlier with Isaiah.

> In the year that King Uzziah died, I saw the Lord seated on a throne, high and exalted, and the train of his robe filled the temple. Above him were seraphs, each with six wings: With two wings they covered their faces, with two they covered

their feet, and with two they were flying. And they were calling to one another:

"Holy, holy, holy is the LORD Almighty; the whole earth is
full of his glory."

At the sound of their voices the doorposts and thresholds
shook and the temple was filled with smoke. (Isa. 6:1–4)

It's interesting that these creatures also had six wings. And as they
flew in the presence of God, they called out the trisagion to each other!
Could it be that Isaiah and John were looking through the same portal,
even though they were separated by centuries of human time?

Both accounts put the trisagion, the thrice holy, right in the
middle of the worship experience going on before the throne.

Maybe you need to ask your worship leader or music minister at
your church, "When are we going to sing the trisagion?"

Maybe he or she will be really impressed that you are using such
a theological word … or maybe your worship leader will look at you
and say, "What on earth is a 'tree-sah-yon'?" For starters you could
say that it's not an "earth word." And then you could describe the
Greek roots of the word and say that simply it's the "thrice holy."

But here's the point:

If the angels, saints, and fantastical creatures are saying and singing it without end in God's presence, maybe we should be praying
and singing it more on earth. What would happen if there was a
patch of earth where this kind of worship unceasingly rose before
the throne? Maybe we would have more profound and transformational God experiences, times when God's presence would come so

strongly that the buildings we are meeting in would shake. We would be unable to carry on with our programs! Wouldn't that be glorious? Not being able to carry on with our lineup of songs, prayers, and rituals, because God came in response to our prayers?

That's an interesting paradox for those of us called to lead in worship. Our highest goal is to be unable to complete what we planned … because God came and took over! We want our seamlessly constructed, smoothly transitioned worship set upset by the glory of the King!

I experienced a taste of that when I wrote this song.

It was the first few days of the year 2006. I had withdrawn to pray for direction … and for a renewing of my heart in worship. I love God with my whole heart, and I love to worship in song, but I was weary of some of the trends I saw in the church's expression of worship: a tendency toward spectacle and performance, a focus on our actions versus the actions of God. As I reflected on what was happening with worship music around the world, one of the desires that grabbed hold of me was the longing for music to help us return to God—that our focus would be less on ourselves and more on God.

I was drawn to the part in Revelation where it describes the constant worship in heaven … and the center of this worship, the powerful trisagion that goes on forever … the "holy, holy, holy." It's as if the angels, saints, and all the heavenly creatures know that holiness is at the very core of who God is. Everything about God emanates from His holiness. Every action of God is motivated by His holiness.

Isn't it interesting that the chant of the creatures wasn't "love, love, love"? Maybe that's ours to do. We are the redeemed who have been forgiven much; perhaps we will sing the *trisagape*[4] forever—a song of the love of God.

But love without holiness can become man centered. That's what so many of the "well-crafted" arguments are filled with these days! Authors and celebrities try to entice us with the notion that we are the center of it all—but it's not true!

God is at the center. And He is HOLY!

And so I dove into the "holy, holy, holy," and I was amazed at how deep the well was ... and is ... and will always be. I realized again that it will take eternity to plumb the depths of who He is. As I meditated on the Scriptures, I realized that I wanted to sing it. Actually "want" is way too weak of a word ... I *had* to sing it! So I began to sing. I spent quite some time singing every "holy" song I could think of—ancient hymns, modern songs—and they were all good ... but they didn't quite satisfy my hunger to sing the "thrice holy."

So I walked over to my piano and began to sing those words with a new melody, like a simple chant. My fingers fell onto a B-flat major chord,[5] and I started by singing a B-flat note falling to an A note ... and pretty soon I was in tears as I sensed the presence of God.

For the first few days all I sang was what is now the chorus ... just the "holy, holy, holy God." And it was enough! It was all I needed to say.

When God comes ... He is all we need.

And so I continued to worship ... until God's presence would come again and I couldn't carry on. And then the silent fullness of God's nearness enveloped me.

Then something interesting started to happen. As I sang the trisagion, I started to hear echoing words, almost like a round. As I would sing the "holy," I would hear (not audibly but in my imagination) a word filling in the space. These words were action words—the actions of God.

That led me to ask this question: "What are the actions of a holy God?" What does Scripture reveal about the character of God through what He is doing?

I knew in my heart this was God's response to the questions and concerns I had over aspects of modern worship ministry. And so the songvision came into view. Lift up a song saturated with the actions of God to counter tendencies that focus on our actions … and center the song around the thrice holy from Revelation and Isaiah. That was the clear and daunting task before me.

So I began filling the air and the page with action words, and the first two that rang true for this emerging song were "creating" and "commanding." I sensed I was heading in the right direction.

Musically the chorus was anchored around the root note and chord to signify that the trisagion is at the center of it all. I then experimented until I found that the right melodic anchor for the action words of the verse was the F note—the fifth degree of the scale.

I then decided that this song would have three verses declaring the actions of God. (Of course, a song built on the thrice holy needed to have three verses!) Once I got rolling, it was actually hard to limit it to three verses because there are so many incredible actions we can attribute solely to God.

The entire story of history is filled with the actions of great men and women, and it's important that we are inspired and challenged by their example. But human actions are finite and often tainted with impure motives. The actions of YHWH are without limit and completely pure. Everything God does, He does out of who He is and for the glory of His name!

Let's meditate on some of the actions of the Holy God as revealed in the Scriptures.

Creating

> In the beginning God created the heavens and the earth.
> (Gen. 1:1)

Everything begins here. This is the action that started it all! If we don't accept that God is our Creator, then nothing in the universe makes sense!

He is the Creator of the universe and everything in it. It takes way more "religious" faith[6] to believe in evolution—that everything happened by chance—than the faith it takes to believe that we were designed and placed here. And as you look into the intricacies of the universe or the human body, it is beyond belief that all these interacting and cooperating systems could have emerged without a designer.

Consider the earth upon which we live. The moon, the closest celestial body to earth, does not have one single living cell on it. Not even one! Yet just one small block of forest soil, a square foot one inch deep, contains an average of 1,356 living creatures: 865 mites, 265 springtails, 22 millipedes, 19 adult beetles, and a various number of over 10 other forms, not to mention another 2 million fungi and algae discernable only by an electron microscope. That's just one small patch of soil in the forest under our feet![7]

Consider the sky and heavens above us. Who doesn't express a sense of awe and wonder when looking up into the silent heavens? The nearest star to planet Earth is our own sun, a mere 93 million miles away. When we observe a sunset, we are watching history: It actually took place eight minutes before we had the pleasure of viewing it—and that's with the view coming at the speed of light! Light travels at the speed of 186,000 miles per second. To help you put that in context, that's about seven times around the equator in a second! That's crazy fast!

The next nearest star to us, the one astronomers named Alpha Centauri, is one of approximately 100 billion stars in our galaxy … and God calls them all by name!

> Lift your eyes and look to the heavens:
> Who created all these?
> He who brings out the starry host one by one,
> *and calls them each by name.*
> Because of his great power and mighty strength,
> not one of them is missing. (Isa. 40:26)

Alpha Centauri is only four light-years from planet Earth. That means we would have to travel fast enough to go around Earth's equator seven times a second and continue at that incomprehensible speed for four years to arrive at the next closest star to us!

Our own galaxy, the Milky Way, has a diameter of about 100,000 light-years. Scientists now estimate that there are about 100 billion galaxies, and those are rapidly expanding—which means either our universe is broadening or we're discovering more of it as our technology advances.[8]

Our God is so overwhelmingly great that many believe He possibly continues to create new and vast regions of outer space, filling them with stars and galaxies—or maybe it's just that what He created in the beginning is so vast we will continue to discover billions and billions of new stars. Either option should put us more in awe of our God!

Yet the "billions and billions" are not just *out there* in the universe. God is also sustaining the billions of tiny cells *in here*, within the human body.

Within the human body's structure of 206 bones and over 700 muscles are more than 30 trillion cells with thousands of unique functions, all performing their tasks within the context of five major systems.[9] The nervous system contains miles of nerve fiber and is controlled by the brain, which performs functions so complex that even the most advanced and powerful computers on earth can't come close to our human intelligence. In the human eye the rods can identify an immensely broad spectrum of light—the most brilliant light perceived is a billion times greater than the dullest light.[10] And—especially important to me as a musician—our ears are amazing (even though they look a little strange). The three tiny bones of the ear can detect sound frequencies so faint they flutter the eardrum one billionth of a centimeter. That's a movement of one-tenth the diameter of a hydrogen atom![11]

Our God worked wonders when He designed and created the universe. And because He is our designer, He has every right to speak into how we live our lives. We are fools if we don't choose to live according to His design. Listen to these powerful words:

> For ever since the world was created, people have seen the earth and sky. Through everything God made, they can clearly see his invisible qualities—his eternal power and divine nature. So they have no excuse for not knowing God.
>
> Yes, they knew God, but they wouldn't worship him as God or even give him thanks. And they began to think up foolish ideas of what God was like. As a result, their minds became dark and confused. Claiming to be wise, they instead became utter fools. And instead of worshiping the glorious, ever-living God, they worshiped idols made to look like mere people and birds and animals and reptiles.
>
> So God abandoned them to do whatever shameful things their hearts desired. As a result, they did vile and degrading things with each other's bodies. They traded the truth about God for a lie. So they worshiped and served the things God created instead of the Creator himself, who is worthy of eternal praise! Amen. (Rom. 1:20–25 NLT)

Because God is our Creator, we are called to acknowledge Him and give Him thanks! We need to thank God for life and everything around us in the natural world that sustains our life—from the air we breathe, to the water we drink, to the food that nourishes our bodies … to the people around us who shelter us with love and provision. And when we don't walk in gratefulness, everything starts to go wrong.

And we have no excuse. I know it's not politically correct to say that people are without excuse—because in our world, it's always someone else's fault!

God shows us the truth. God speaks the truth.

Commanding

I chose *commanding* as the second action of God to highlight in this song for several reasons. Lyrically it was another word starting with *c*. Using alliteration—the repetition of a consonant sound, especially in a song that may have any type of list—helps us remember what is coming next. But most importantly, I used *commanding* because it speaks of God speaking: the way He creates, the way He rules through His spoken word.

> In the beginning God created the heavens and the earth. Now the earth was formless and empty, darkness was over the surface of the deep, and the Spirit of God was hovering over the waters.
>
> *And God said, "Let there be light," and there was light.*
> (Gen. 1:1–3)

God does everything by speaking it out. He created the universe with the Word, and He still speaks today!

There is an incredible parallel between Genesis 1 and John 1—very strong evidence that the Holy Spirit was guiding the authors of Scripture.

> In the beginning was the Word, and the Word was with God,
> and the Word was God. He was with God in the beginning.
> Through him all things were made; without him noth-
> ing was made that has been made. (John 1:1–3)

God commanded the universe into existence—and God is still commanding today. Sometimes our word pictures paint God as too soft, as a gentleman who never commands authority. Yes, God invites us and doesn't force us to love Him. He gives us complete freedom to accept or reject Him. But He is still the Almighty, the One who speaks things into being, the One who is fully in charge.

Transcendent

He who is creating and commanding is the transcendent Adonai. He is the Holy One of Israel. The Holy God first revealed Himself to Israel and made a covenant with it. Since the coming of Jesus, He does not belong to any one nation[12] but to all who worship Him and follow the Lamb.

Transcendence speaks of "otherness." Transcendence reminds us that God is beyond us—and so we are not to worship anyone or anything created. God is not like us. We are made in God's image; He is not made in ours.

> You shall have no other gods before me.
> You shall not make for yourself an idol in the form of
> anything in heaven above or on the earth beneath or in the

waters below. You shall not bow down to them or worship them; for I, the LORD your God, am a jealous God. (Ex. 20:3–5)

Out of reverence for the holiness of God, devout Jews would not say the name of God—what the theologians call the "tetragrammaton"[13]—YHWH. Instead they would say, "Adonai," which means "Lord." Your Bible translates Adonai by putting the word *Lord* in small capital letters.

This God defends love. His power doesn't simply overpower all who oppose Him—it's used to defend all that is good.

And when He needs to, our Holy God will destroy sin and all wickedness that rise up against Him.

Warrior

I wanted to include some of the terrifying actions of God in this song because I wanted us to sing out some of the strong and robust biblical images of the character and actions of God.

Our God is a warrior. He is not a wimp. Just because He is patient does not mean He is weak.

Our Holy God was not created by some people sitting around intellectualizing about the concept of God. He is a God of action, and He is not afraid to use His power to accomplish His purposes!

Some people have tried to portray the Almighty as one who goes around in a rancorous rage, making everyone's life miserable. They believe He crafts His commands to kill our fun. Nothing could be further from the truth. In fact His commands are designed to release us into joy and protect us from harm. Delivering judgment or discipline breaks His heart. He longs for the rebellious to turn back and be saved. But if people refuse to repent, He will release His wrath. Remember that all have had countless opportunities to turn to God. Just living on planet Earth and seeing the qualities of a Creator all around us provide evidence enough of who He is and what He asks of us. And so God's judgments are always just.

He will destroy sin, for no sin and impurity can dwell in the presence of a holy God.

Forgiving

But how does a holy God destroy sin?

Here is where it starts getting really surprising as we meditate on the actions of God: This Holy God with immeasurable power and glory limited Himself and went through the incarnation so that He could walk among us. And why would He do such an outrageous thing? As our Creator, He is brokenhearted when we are separated from His holy presence by sin. He knows that He alone is the source of all good things and that we are meant to dwell in His presence. He knows that our own effort is never enough to restore us to His holy presence (even though the religions of the world keep on trying!).

So the eternal, unbroken fellowship of the triune God was broken as Jesus, the Son of God, was sent to Earth—not just as Yeshua, the Messiah for the Jews, but as Jesus, the Savior for every tribe and tongue.

Our Holy God sets out to forgive and redeem from every tribe, tongue, nation, and culture!

Arising

Here's how He did it! The death and resurrection of Jesus is the central and most important act of humanity. That's what I chose to declare in the last line of verse two, the middle of the song:

> Arising first
> The nail-scarred Lamb
> Salvation's champion

He is the champion of champions. And what is He the champion of?

Salvation!

Eternal and true—He is everything we have ever needed and longed for. He is salvation's champion.

While working on this book, I watched some of the 2008 Summer Olympics. One of the big stories of the 2008 Games was Michael Phelps. It's interesting to find out the background of some of these athletes and what motivates them. Michael's father left when he was only seven years old (a story far too common in our modern world), and Michael's mother alone raised Michael and his two sisters. Debbie Phelps has been Michael's biggest fan and supporter through all of his training, and like all good moms, she has been present at all his big swimming contests and races.

During the Olympic coverage, the cameras would often go back and forth between Michael in the pool and his mother in the stands. One of the times, as I watched Debbie watch her son, I was reminded of another mother watching her son in a great contest: Mary the mother of Jesus was there at the foot of the cross.[14] And while Debbie Phelps watched her son emerge victorious, it may have seemed to Mary that her son lost the contest on that day. But that was because none in the frightened cluster of supporters huddled with Mary at the foot of cross nor any of the Roman soldiers who callously carried out the execution could see the scope of the whole battle! After Jesus faithfully remained on the brutal cross through excruciating pain and suffering, He declared these three words into the seen and unseen world: *It is finished.* "The contest is over, and I am the victor! Even though the whole world thinks I failed, and all the demonic powers think they have defeated Me, I will emerge the victor yet!"

And what happened early on that Sunday morning proved His victory!

Can you imagine what the victory celebrations are going to be like when every tribe and tongue get to unleash all of their joy and devotion on the One who has redeemed them?

Through His death and resurrection, Jesus became the champion of champions!

The *Australian* described Michael Phelps at the height of the 2008 Games as the "champion who swims in his own galaxy." Those are heady words for a mere mortal who merely swims well, albeit incredibly well. Michael Phelps may be the champion of the Olympic swimming pool for a few years[15], but his galaxy is pretty small compared to Jesus'—Jesus is the champion who created the galaxies!

And somewhere out there beyond the galaxies He created, in a completely different realm, the Lamb of God now stands in the center of the throne of God.

And He is worshipped … for He is worthy to be worshipped!

And all the saints, elders, and the creatures lift up the trisagion—the thrice holy. And as they do, they are holding out mystery and revelation.

There is something about this thrice holy that reveals the triune God. He is Three—yet only One. He is in eternal relationship, a community of love and fellowship of life. Some theologians called the trinity a "circle dance."

Brenton Brown and I have cowritten a song called "Triune God." We wrote it out of the sense that God's people need more songs that convey the theology and truth of the triune nature of God. We actually wrote the song in "three" (3/4 or 6/8 time) so that the very fabric of the music underpinning the words would convey this nature and relationship.

Triune God

Triune God
Uncreated
Perfect Three in One

Sacred bond
Humble friendship

Living dance of light
Draw our lives into the wonder of Your

Majesty
Your fellowship divine
The Spirit's liberty
The grace of Jesus Christ
The Father's faithful love
The sharing of Your life
In holy communion
One God[16]

A living dance of light. A dance of love and relationship.

A theologian from the seventh century, John of Damascus, was the first person to talk of the triune God this way. He described the Trinity as a "pericoresis" (perry-co-ray-sis). This Greek word comes from *peri*, meaning "around," and *choresis,* meaning "dancing." Listen to what he wrote:

> *Father, Son and Holy Spirit are like three dancers, holding hands, dancing together in perfect love, perfect freedom and perfect harmony. They are deeply one yet they are three. They are unified in one intimate, indissoluble substance, yet they are recognizable community. Most importantly, they are what they are only in relationship to one another—in shared purpose, and in mutual love that is expressed through each other for eternity.*[17]

It's a mystery, a wonder that we will explore throughout eternity—this triune God in perpetual loving relationship. And this God not only created us. He not only redeems us. He does all of this for an extraordinary end!

We would think that God, who is holy and pure, would keep His distance from us and our world, polluted with sin and impurities as it is. God, who is perfect and holy, draws near to humanity to forgive and redeem, even to the point of sending His only Son, the "nail-scarred Lamb," to pay the price for our rebellion.

Romancing

But He doesn't stop there! His goal is not just for our forgiveness so we can become His loyal subjects and servants—God is actually romancing us!

I took a big risk using the word *romancing* in a worship song describing the Holy God. When I use that word, I am not referring to the sweet, selfish, sentimental concept that is popular in our culture. I use the word in the biggest, grandest God sense. God is the one who is drawing us, inviting us, and lavishing us with expressions of love and kindness—just look at the beauty of creation all around us, even in its fallen state! God is courting and romancing us with one aim: so that we may freely return that love and become devoted lovers of God. He is the one who created romance. Romance is rooted in the "forsaking all others" union of marriage, the covenantal relationship designed to be a source of blessing and revelation.

As a lover, God pursues us and reclaims us, not to use us and leave us, but to restore us to our created purpose. And then He sets us free in our hearts to live transformed lives, which brings life, not only to ourselves but also to all those around us. The more we focus on who God is, the more we become who we were meant to be.

Roar

At the end of the song, I chose to use the powerful audio image of "The Lion's mighty roar" because I wanted to be clear whom the One romancing us is not someone small and cute that we can control like a domesticated house cat! No, the One drawing us is awesome, intriguing, and fully in charge ... like C. S. Lewis's Aslan! Our love relationship with God will never be tame and safe. We can't predict and control Him.

He is after all HOLY, HOLY, HOLY!

But we can trust our Great Romancer because He is good. Isn't it awesome that we get to spend our lives worshipping this kind of God?

Let's return to John on the isle of Patmos. As he got lost in this open vision, he was filled with the presence of God. He surrendered again to Jesus, the resurrected, nail-scarred Lamb, salvation's champion. And he wrote on a scroll everything he saw and experienced.

We don't know exactly how much time John spent on Patmos after he wrote the whole vision down. Months? Years? However long it was, I am sure his heart was full each day as he relived the vision and basked in the presence of God. And he waited for deliverance—either for his body to give out so he could be present with his Lord, or for a political change in Rome to set him free. The change came in AD 96. Back in Rome the emperor Domitian met his end just like he feared. He was so paranoid that he had multiple mirrors installed in every room in his palace so he could always see an attacker coming. If he got wind that someone opposed him, he had them executed—or if he couldn't kill them, he exiled them as he exiled John. But on September 18 in AD 96, his mirrors were not enough to save him. An assassin, Stephanus, was able to slip through his guard and take his life.

John was now free to return to Ephesus, where he would spend his last days ministering and being ministered to. But he brought something from the island with him … a scroll, with three words in the center.

Holy … holy … holy.

SONGWRITING TIPS

Try writing in a new key, as long as the songvision and content match the key. Some believe that each key has its own personality and is a good match for certain subjects. Apparently Handel thought that key signatures with five, six, seven, or eight sharps were "transcendental" keys, which he associated with heaven. He used particular chords to awaken certain feelings—G minor to evoke urgency or jealousy; E minor to create a sorrowful, lamenting mood; G major to create moods reminiscent of bright sunlight and green pastures; F minor to provoke gloom and despondency.

I don't take all of those key descriptions that literally, but I do believe that key signatures play a role in the emotional content of a song.

Anchor your melody with a key note and motif. I built the chorus of this song around the B-flat to A notes, a descending pattern for the word "holy." Repetition of your key notes and motif is vital to other people being able to sing the song you are writing.

Use alliteration to help people remember the words. The first verse of "Holy God" is built upon words starting with c ("creating, commanding") and phrases starting with d ("defending love, destroying sin"). When you are writing your song, make sure to see if you can use alliteration to strengthen the lyrics and make them easier to remember.

Take risks lyrically—use some bold words to surprise and stir up hearts and emotions. I do this every time I write a song. I try to keep stretching and experimenting. Language can be quite stimulating and provocative in a good way. It should stir us up. It should be inflammatory! I am so tired of nice songs with nice platitudes. Take some risks as you write, and keep your risks anchored in truth!

Notes

1. "Holy God" by Brian Doerksen © 2006 Integrity's Hosanna! Music/ASCAP & Shining Rose Songs (adm by Integrity's Hosanna! Music)/ASCAP. Used by permission.

2. Somewhere between AD 81 and AD 95.

3. "Domitian," Encyclopaedia Britannica, http://www.britannica.com/EBchecked/topic/168802/Domitian (accessed April 15, 2009).

4. I made that word up, so don't try to find it in other theological writings!

5. Most of us songwriters have favorite keys—places on our guitars or piano that just feel natural to us. For me, my big keys are F, C, D, E, and A. I don't write that much in G (though I have), and I don't think I'd ever written a song in B-flat before writing "Holy God"! The original recording is in B-flat; my second recording is in B, a really bright and bold key also good for conveying transcendence like one of my other cowritten songs "Everlasting"!

6. What I mean by "religious" faith is faith in the unverifiable—that's what makes it faith! How can they verify what may have happened millions of years ago?

7. Dr. Paul Brand and Philip Yancey, *Fearfully and Wonderfully Made* (Grand Rapids, MI: Zondervan, 1987), 21.

8. Oliver E. Summers, *What Is God Up To?—Why Earth?—Why Eternity?* (Longwood, FL: Xulon Press, 2008), 26.

9. Ruth E. McCall and Cathee M. Tankersley, *Phlebotomy Essentials* (Philadelphia, PA: Lippincott, Williams, and Wilkins, 2007), 138.

10. Donald Kennedy, comp., *From Cell to Organism: Readings from* Scientific American (San Francisco: W. H. Freeman, 1967), 152.

11. Ibid., 132.

12. But His covenant with Israel as a people remains!

13. The tetragrammaton is Greek. *Tetra* means "four," and *grammaton* means "letters." This four-letter symbol for God appears almost 7,000 times in the Hebrew Scriptures. ("Tetragrammaton," www.wikipedia.com, accessed April 14, 2009.)

14. I have often wondered what happened to Joseph. For him not to be there at the cross must have meant that he had already died. I just can't comprehend any other reason for him not to be present!

15. Sometime after the Olympics, a picture of Michael made the news again—this time catching him smoking pot at a party. Seems like this "champion" still has some things to learn out of the swimming pool!

16. "Triune God" by Brian Doerksen & Brenton Brown © 2005 Integrity's Hosanna! Music/ASCAP & Shining Rose Songs (adm by Integrity's Hosanna! Music)/ASCAP & Thankyou Music (adm by worshiptogether.com Songs). Used by permission.

17. John of Damascus, *De Fide Orthodoxa,* i. 8, p. 94, 829A.

Father, I Want You to Hold Me

Father, I want You to hold me
I want to rest in Your arms today
Father, I want You to show me
How much You care for me in every way

I bring all my cares
And I lay them at Your feet
You are always there
And You love me as I am
Yes You love me as I am

Father, I know You will hold me
I know I am Your child, Your own
Father, I know You will show me
I feel Your arms holding me, I'm not alone

I bring all my fears
And I lay them at Your feet
You are always here
And You love me as I am
Yes You love me as I am[1]

CHAPTER 3

Father, I Want You to Hold Me

It was October 1988. My wife, Joyce, and I were out near Tofino, British Columbia, on the extreme west coast of Canada where the rain forest meets the mighty Pacific Ocean on Vancouver Island. It's a place unlike any other on the planet. I was making Joyce really nervous as I bounded from one large rock to another, the surf pounding all around me. Joyce's nerves had nothing to do with me, though. She was worried about the bundle I had strapped to my chest in a carrier—our first baby daughter, Rachel Noelle Doerksen, who was all of three months old. When we look at family pictures on family night, a picture from that trip occasionally comes up, and Joyce gives me the look: "What were you thinking?" And my response: "I don't have a clue. I guess I was just enjoying the moment and not thinking about the danger ... and just maybe we spend too much time thinking about the dangers in our modern life of health and safety." Joyce's look still persists, but I know Rachel was always safe that day—because I was holding her.

It was our first trip away as parents—young parents that we were, all of twenty-three years old. It was on this trip that I wrote "Father, I Want You to Hold Me." This was to become my very first published song, and I guess in many ways it started me on a journey that I am still on today.

During my childhood and teenage years, I had a deep craving for affection. Maybe it started with my whole birth experience, as my first few weeks of life were anything but normal.

Here is how my dad describes my entrance into this world and how I spent my first few weeks of life:

> It was the middle of November 1965. I was fully involved in my assignment at South Poplar Elementary, teaching a grade 5 class. We were expecting the birth of our second child any day. Names had been chosen, and now it was just a matter of time before we would know if God was giving us a girl or another boy. On Wednesday, November 17, I left for school as usual. It was during that day that Agnes realized the moment of her delivery was near. She went to MSA hospital in Abbotsford. My mother, Tina Doerksen, was called to look after Allen, our twenty-two-month-old son. Once I arrived home from my school assignment, she went home, and I prepared supper for Allen and myself. In the meantime I received the news that Agnes was in labor and all things seemed to be going smoothly. In those days men were not

allowed to be with their wives during delivery. After supper I was told that Agnes had given birth at 7:30 p.m. to a healthy boy weighing in at nine pounds, nine ounces. I phoned family with the happy news and asked my mother to come back and look after Allen, giving me opportunity to visit Agnes briefly and view the new arrival. By the time I arrived at the hospital, it was after 8 p.m. Agnes looked so relaxed and happy, and we rejoiced together and named our little bundle after I saw him behind the glass: Brian Robert. Driving home, I was elated; it felt like "walking on cloud nine." It was so easy to speak thanksgiving to the Father.

The next morning was hectic. Allen had to be looked after and prepared for the day, phone calls had to be made, etc. Mother arrived at 8:15 a.m. to be with Allen while I was on my way to South Poplar Elementary. There was plenty of excitement as I shared the news with the staff. I had barely started the first lesson of the day when my principal, Paul Dyck, walked into my classroom and whispered to me to take the phone in the office. It was Dr. Woods' office (our doctor) calling that I needed to come to the hospital immediately to see Agnes before they took her via ambulance to St. Paul's hospital in Vancouver.

She was in a coma.

As I hung up the phone, fear gripped me to

such an extent that I could hardly talk or walk. I
made my way back to the classroom and informed
the principal of what had just transpired. He told
me to leave for the hospital immediately. I quickly
explained to him my teaching plans for the day
and then was on my way. At that time we drove
a 1953 Ford. As I left school, it dawned on me
that I might have to follow the ambulance to
Vancouver. I didn't really trust our car to drive on
the new freeway at high speed following an ambu-
lance, so I stopped at the George Lepp residence
on Hawthorne, just past what is now Central
Heights Church, and exchanged our Ford for
their 1964 Ford. As I approached MSA hospital,
the ambulance was ready to leave for Vancouver
with Agnes inside. I was to follow. What an ago-
nizing drive that was, traveling at 85 mph (137
km/h) on the freeway. Of course, traffic in those
days was nothing like today. I was just glad it
wasn't raining. My thoughts were in total confu-
sion. There were moments I feared I would not
see Agnes alive again. Then I started to accuse
God of teasing me by reminding me of how He
had brought her into my life and how He was tak-
ing her away after three years and some months.
The Enemy taunted me that I did not deserve a
wife of her caliber and therefore I was receiving
what was coming to me. My body became numb

to the extent that my hands, white in appearance, felt frozen to the steering wheel. To be in such a condition while driving at high speed was very dangerous. I started to plead with God to take me and give our two boys their mother back. Once at St. Paul's hospital, Agnes was rushed into intensive care. I was not allowed to see her. All I could do was pace the hallway in deep emotional agony, being tormented by the Enemy (although I didn't recognize it at the time). After what seemed like a long time, Dr. McNaughten, the head specialist, came down to see me. His words were like a knife to my stomach: "I'm sorry, but I cannot give you any hope for your wife to make it. Please call the family." He then added that if I believed in prayer, this would be a good time to pray. I was numb and said nothing. Once he left me I did make an effort to phone someone in the family and asked them to call all the others. As I waited that day into the evening, I expected to be called any moment to say my good-bye. But it didn't happen, so I went home for the night.

The following two days became a blur in my life. I lost all sense of time and couldn't keep schedules. I hardly ate or slept. People tried to comfort me, but I heard little. It all seemed like a bad dream or nightmare. I couldn't cry and hardly spoke a word. The Enemy pounded me into the ground. I carried unbelievable guilt for something I couldn't put my finger on.

I believe it was into the second day when Dr. McNaughten spoke to me and shared his disbelief that Agnes hadn't died yet. He then added that if she didn't die she would be a vegetable because the brain cannot endure the pressure and high temperature that she'd experienced. Those were no comforting words.

It was on the third day that the miracle revealed itself. That afternoon Agnes woke from her coma unexpectedly, creating a flurry of activities around her bed in the intensive care unit. It didn't take long before the doctor knew she wasn't a vegetable. Her mind was clear. The miracle was complete. She had to stay in St. Paul's for almost two weeks, which made it very difficult for me to keep everything going with Allen at home, Brian in MSA hospital, and myself at South Poplar Elementary. But that was a small price to pay for the miracle that God had handed me.

Once at home, Agnes was not allowed to do anything. Brian also came home, finally feeling the touch of his mother over two weeks after his birth, no longer being looked after by female patients in the hospital. We had help come every day while I was at school. Once home, I ran the household.

This meant every night for the next four to six weeks I'd get up at 3:30 a.m. and feed Brian a bottle. He was a very good baby. It was a great bonding time. I believe it was when he was six weeks old and sleeping in his crib that I bent over him one night and dedicated him to the Lord, not knowing what the future would hold for him and for us. —Harry Doerksen

What a way to enter the world! My dad doesn't mention it in his account, but when he arrived at St. Paul's hospital, the nurses were so sure that my mom wouldn't make it, they placed her personal belongings in the morgue! (How's that for confidence in their ability to save her life!)

I'm so glad that God answered those desperate prayers and kept my mother alive. To this day we are very close—and my mom is an intercessor, so it could very well be that I'm alive because of some of the prayers she has prayed for me!

But what was the effect of this whole ordeal on me? I spent most of my first weeks being passed from nurse to nurse and left in a baby cot behind the glass until I squalled loudly enough. I couldn't talk or let them know how I was feeling about this whole arrangement, other than with my tears and cries. I am sure I couldn't understand why I wasn't with my mother. I wasn't breast-fed, and I didn't have a chance to bond with my mother in the way babies are designed to bond. The doctors also tied up my mother's tubes after this, so I was the last child in our family even though I was only number two.

This is how I started my life.

When God created human beings, He made us need and even crave physical touch. We have all heard about the cruel experiments done on babies where touch was withheld from them—we simply are not created to function without lots of loving, affirming touch. And of course, in recent years, we have discovered in prayer ministry and in counseling and modern psychology that what happens in our mother's womb and in the first days and weeks of our lives can impact us deeply over our whole lives.

And so I remember distinctly longing for both my mother's and my father's affirmation and affection as a boy. The challenge was that my mom and dad were busy, as most parents are! On top of that my dad was raised by his German-speaking, Mennonite mother to believe that showing emotion is weakness. As I became an adult, I got to know my parents and the story of the Doerksen and Unger lines better. I heard stories of what they suffered in Russia and how they fled the Russian revolution; the Ungers ended up in the Canadian prairies, and Peter Doerksen, my grandpa, ended up in Paraguay in what was called the "green hell."[2] As a result, I appreciated more the need they had to be tough and unemotional. But I was not living in the green hell or fleeing Russians … I was growing up in the 1970s on the west coast of Canada, and I needed emotional affection and affirmation. One of the ways I compensated in high school was having a few girlfriends—probably not because I was ready for a serious relationship, but simply because I was craving affection. Thankfully I got to know my wife-to-be while in high school too. I actually met her when I was twelve years old. It was the first day of high school at MEI—a private Mennonite high school in Abbotsford, British Columbia. Joyce was also a Doerksen, though thankfully an unrelated one as there were *many* Doerksens in the area. I took one look at her and said to myself, "She's going to be my wife one day."

On a long weekend in May 1981, my parents were away for several days of music ministry with the Ambassadors Quartet. I put together a party and invited a bunch of people, including Joyce and her girlfriends, but Joyce was the catch I was after! I dragged my parents' stereo all the way up to the middle of the field behind our house. (Music is important, you know!) We had a big bonfire and listened to loud music. At one point that night, I sat down beside her, and we looked up into the starry sky together … and, well, she just couldn't resist me anymore! We started dating that summer and got married in November 1984, one week after I turned nineteen so I could sign my own marriage certificate as an adult.

Now fast-forward to when I became a father for the first time. The first of our six children, Rachel, arrived on August 8, 1988 (8/8/88!). I was both delighted and scared to death. There was a moment that I shared with Rachel on the west coast of Vancouver Island that changed everything for me. She looked up at me with those big brown eyes and held her arms out, and without words she said, "Daddy … I want you to hold me." And so I held her—and suddenly the tears and a realization came to me: "This is what I always wanted to say to my earthly father … and ultimately to my heavenly Father: Father, I want you to hold me." And so in that moment I scrolled through my mental Rolodex[3] of songs to see if I could recall a single one that expressed that desire … and I couldn't think of any! So with my baby daughter beside me, I picked up my guitar and began to find a way to sing that cry back to God. Remember, at this point, I hadn't written a song before (other than a handful of songs that I wrote as part of a Christian garage band called Lodestar when I was a teenager); I'd never thought that I had the gifting or calling to be a songwriter. And as I wrote a few phrases and started singing them back to God, I kept experiencing waves of God's presence washing over me. So I started and finished the song in the few days we shared as a new family beside the ocean in October 1988. This was my secret song to God. Often during devotions, or when I would go for a walk and my thoughts would turn to God or to my daughter Rachel, I would sing this song. I think the only other person who heard the song was my wife, Joyce.

Sometime later in one of our local-church home groups, after someone shared on the Father-heart of God, Andy Park (who was the worship pastor of our church, the Langley Vineyard) turned and encouraged me to share an appropriate song. As I remember it, he said, "Brian, I think you have a song that would be right for this moment." I sensed it was time for my secret song to become public (at least with those twenty people), and so I shared it. I remember being *really* nervous and anxious that this song would seem rather silly to others because it was my private song to God; however, it actually seemed to touch people and bring them close to God. Several people came up afterward to thank me, amazed that I had written such a timely song. That was a totally new experience for me.

A few months later I was playing bass guitar on Andy Park's worship team at a John Wimber and Vineyard Ministries conference in Edmonton. After Ed Piorek spoke a powerful message on the Father-heart of God, Andy was called up to close the session with a song. Instead of heading for the platform, Andy turned to me and said, "You go do that 'Father' song you shared that night in the home group." I had been apprehensive playing the song for twenty people … and now Andy wanted me to play it for several thousand! And so I nervously walked up onto the stage and sang the song, and people began to weep—and I don't mean just a few tears. People really began to weep as the Spirit of God opened up the "father-wound" in their hearts and the song gave voice to the heart's cry. After the service was over, John Wimber came up to me (I think this was the first time we spoke directly), and he said something like, "Thanks for that powerful song. When I was a young boy, my alcoholic father left, and you just put into song what I have wanted to say to my Father in heaven my whole life. Could we publish this song?" I was humbled and grateful and then said something like, "What do you mean by 'publish'?" I had no clue!

Later that year Vineyard did record and publish my "private" song. It's not my most recognized song, but it's still one of my personal favorites because it invites us to come as we are, enter the Father's house, and experience unconditional love!

The words of Jesus in John 14 are full of life and truth: "I will not leave you as orphans…. My Father will love him, and we will come to him and make our home with him" (vv. 18, 23).

The Father loves. Worship is receiving that love.

The Father comes to make His home with us. Worship is letting Him draw near and dwell with us.

I believe that worship begins with what we receive, not with what we give.

Receiving the Father's love is one of the crucial foundations of a life of worship. If we don't truly know we are loved unconditionally as a son or daughter, we will gravitate toward religious performance in our worship.

Religion is built through performance and focus on keeping people in a culture of appearances and comparisons. I just heard in the news today that there is a new morality police in the Palestinian territories; they move through public places, making sure everyone observes Ramadan correctly. The morality police in our culture and churches don't wear official uniforms, but they're always there, silently or loudly scolding people who are not measuring up.

But the Father is moving among us not to scold us for the ways in which we fail, but to invite us to live in the "glorious freedom of the children of God" (Rom. 8:21).

It's true that the revelation of the Father-heart of God is desperately needed in the Muslim countries of the world. But we need the Father's love in every nation—because when we see God as the good Father He really is, we are freed to worship the Father in spirit and truth.

As we see the Father, we are freed from fatherless worship.

This is so powerfully illustrated in the parable of the two lost sons and their wastefully extravagant father in Luke 15.

> To illustrate the point further, Jesus told them this story: "A man had two sons. The younger son told his father, 'I want my share of your estate now before you die.' So his father agreed to divide his wealth between his sons.
>
> "A few days later this younger son packed all his belongings and moved to a distant land, and there he wasted all his money in wild living. About the time his money ran out, a great famine swept over the land, and he began to starve.

He persuaded a local farmer to hire him, and the man sent him into his fields to feed the pigs. The young man became so hungry that even the pods he was feeding the pigs looked good to him. But no one gave him anything.

"When he finally came to his senses, he said to himself, 'At home even the hired servants have food enough to spare, and here I am dying of hunger! I will go home to my father and say, "Father, I have sinned against both heaven and you, and I am no longer worthy of being called your son. Please take me on as a hired servant."'

"So he returned home to his father. And while he was still a long way off, his father saw him coming. Filled with love and compassion, he ran to his son, embraced him, and kissed him. His son said to him, 'Father, I have sinned against both heaven and you, and I am no longer worthy of being called your son.'

"But his father said to the servants, 'Quick! Bring the finest robe in the house and put it on him. Get a ring for his finger and sandals for his feet. And kill the calf we have been fattening. We must celebrate with a feast, for this son of mine was dead and has now returned to life. He was lost, but now he is found.' So the party began.

"Meanwhile, the older son was in the fields working. When he returned home, he heard music and dancing in the house, and he asked one of the servants what was going on. 'Your brother is back,' he was told, 'and your father has killed the fattened calf. We are celebrating because of his safe return.'

"The older brother was angry and wouldn't go in. His father came out and begged him, but he replied, 'All these years I've slaved for you and never once refused to do a single thing you told me to. And in all that time you never gave me even one young goat for a feast with my friends. Yet when this son of yours comes back after squandering your money on prostitutes, you celebrate by killing the fattened calf!'

"His father said to him, 'Look, dear son, you have always stayed by me, and everything I have is yours. We had to celebrate this happy day. For your brother was dead and has come back to life! He was lost, but now he is found!'" (Luke 15:11–32 NLT)

But how many of us would prefer that the story ended differently, perhaps something like this?

The younger son returned, and he was punished and made to work for ten years to pay off his debt. The father realized he had never truly acknowledged all the years of faithful, steady service from his oldest son, so he threw a big thank-you party in the eldest son's honor (partly to increase the younger son's guilt and to motivate him to be good from now on).

And this is the way the first hearers would have expected this story to end. There is evidence that a story much like this was already circulating in that part of the world.

But Jesus didn't tell the story this way. He ended the story with the wasteful extravagance of grace!

And to this day waste is still offensive to the religious. Grace is beyond comprehension to those who pride themselves on their own track record.

The elder brother's words reveal the heart of fatherless worship:

> But he answered his father, "Look! *All these years* I've been *slaving for you* and *never disobeyed your orders.* Yet *you never gave me* even a young goat so I could celebrate with my friends. But when this *son of yours* who has *squandered* your property with prostitutes comes home, you kill the fattened calf for him!"

All these years—words that speak clearly of the elder son's self-effort to climb the religious ladder of performance: "It's who I am and what I have done that's important." *All these years*—three words together that sound so weary.

And then he uses a word that never crossed the father's mind: *slaving.* This was never the father's desire.

In the musical version of this story called *Prodigal God*[4] that I have cowritten with Christopher Greco, the Prodigal Son sings this when he reaches rock bottom and starts to come to his senses:

> *"In my father's house, there are no slaves; only servants and sons."*

His father never wanted either of his sons to slave for him. Serving is a good thing; slaving speaks of bondage. Serving is the Father's way; slaving is the Enemy's way.

And then the older son says something that proves he is a liar. He says that he *never disobeyed*. It makes you wonder—how did this son manage to be so perfect? How did he manage that when no one else in history—other than the One telling the story—ever managed it?

The older brother essentially says in this grand claim, "It's my track record that counts, not who my father is." This is Javert in the classic book, movie, and musical *Les Misérables*. Javert's choices are one of the clearest portrayals of where this kind of thinking leads. For this kind of person, life is all about following orders in the chain of command. Yes, it's true that the father had authority and could give orders—and at times needed to—but what happened to relationship? What happened to the sense of privilege in the son serving his father's desire?

And then the older son uses the language of distance: *But when this "son of yours" … comes home.* He doesn't call him "my brother," for he wants nothing to do with him. He made that very clear by not going in to the party!

The next word that comes out of his mouth is a powerful word— the word that is translated in most English Bibles as *squandered*. Can you hear the disdain dripping from his mouth as he says that word? For people who strive religiously, other people's waste is very offensive to them. He was deeply offended at his brother's waste and his father's grace. He hated his father's wasteful extravagance!

And then he lies again: *Yet you never gave me …*

He says these words to his father's face!

But if we look back to Luke 15:12 for just a moment, we read: "He divided his property between them." The word *them* means that the father gave each son his share. The younger son took his money and ran; the elder son—the son who was religious and afraid—ran away in his heart, too afraid to act out his inner desires. He stayed home physically, but his heart was far away from his father.

I identify deeply with the older son. Like many others who grew up in the church, I have sometimes wanted to run far away, sometimes thought that those in the world have way more fun than those of us in the church.

And as in the story of the older son, my Father has given me everything—yet I forget so quickly, complaining when God pours out His goodness and mercy on someone who, from my flawed and limited perspective, simply does not deserve it!

The story that Jesus told ends with the father pleading with the elder brother out in the field. Jesus doesn't tell His listeners whether he ever softens his heart toward his brother and returns home to his father in his heart.

In the musical that Christopher and I wrote, we have imagined and brought to life the turning of the elder son as the climax of our story sometime after the prodigal's return. How that happens I don't have space to tell you in this book; you will have to experience it when you hear or see the musical.[5]

When we worship the Father, we can begin just like the Prodigal Son—by expressing our need. I started this song with the words *Father, I want You to hold me.* In worship we start where we are, but we don't end there.

God responds. God comes. God changes us.

Worship moves us to a place of resting in His love. That's why the second verse of this song starts with *Father, I know You will hold me.*

I know that I am a child of the Father … and deeper than my feelings is my identity, and deeper than my identity is who my Father is.

He is the perfect combination of authority and affection, of wisdom and compassion. He is generous and good. He is approachable yet holy.

He is the Father all of us have been searching for!

At the end of each letter I write, I sign off with this little phrase: *In the Father's love.*

That's how I want to live my life—in the Father's love. That's the place I anchor my worship—in the Father's love. That's where I will spend eternity—in the Father's love.

SONGWRITING TIPS

Write secret songs to God! Write songs that are only for God's ears. In a way all of our worship songs should start that way. A worship songwriter once told me, "I want to write a song that the church around the world will sing." Sounds grand and great! But actually it sounds like pride. My suggestion to emerging writers is simply this: Instead of trying to write a song that the church will sing, start by writing a song that you want to sing in secret to God. Write the song that you have the guts to sing in secret when no one else but God will hear you! Don't bypass your own heart by just trying to write for the church. If you bypass your own heart and life, your song will sound plastic and lack authenticity.

Let God bring you forward—don't promote yourself and your own songs. This is a really challenging area. You could move through seasons when it is time to be bold and share what God has given you. But don't start there. Start in a place of hiddenness and service. God knows what you have written, and He is fully able to call it forward at the right time and in the right place.

Use honest, earthy words to express your desire for God. I have been accused over the years of being too intimate with my songs, and "Father, I Want You to Hold Me" was the first that triggered that accusation. It's an indictment that I gladly answer, "Guilty as charged." I believe we were created for intimacy with God, and for way too long we have been too artificial in our worship song lyrics.

Write the unique songs that spring out of your life. Don't worry about being universal too quickly. Just say the unique thing that comes to you, and later you can discern whether the song is truly just for you or whether it's meant to serve others as well.

Notes

1. Brian Doerksen, "Father, I Want You to Hold Me," © 1989 Vineyard Songs Canada and ION Publishing. Used by permission.

2. One of the highlights of the last few years was taking my dad back to his place of birth in Paraguay and seeing the green hell for myself; it's quite amazing how the Mennonites have made a life in a very hot and inhospitable land.

3. If you're under thirty, you probably don't have a clue what a Rolodex is!

4. We are using *Prodigal God* as our title for the musical because this is who God is. The word *prodigal* means "wastefully extravagant." The elder son begins by seeing his father's extravagance as a negative thing, but through a series of circumstances and his own choices, he transforms, realizing that it is a good thing.

5. At the time of writing, we have released an initial five-song EP (available for free for a limited time) and are preparing for a full-length recording of the songs and a concert tour of the musical with a live band and actors. We are also considering a novel version of the script and, down the road, maybe even a film of it. The free EP and updates will be posted on the musical Web site (www.prodigal-god.com) and on my Web site (www.BrianDoerksen.com).

Refiner's Fire

Purify my heart, let me be as gold
And precious silver
Purify my heart, let me be as gold
pure gold

Refiner's fire, my heart's one desire
Is to be holy, set apart for You Lord
I choose to be holy
Set apart for You my Master
Ready to do Your will

Purify my heart, cleanse me from within
And make me holy
Purify my heart, cleanse me from my sin
Deep within[1]

CHAPTER 4

Refiner's Fire

It was a warm summer day in 1989, a typical day in my life as the new worship pastor of the Langley Vineyard Christian Fellowship in British Columbia, Canada. I was all of twenty-three years old. We lived close to our church offices, so I returned home to see my wife, Joyce, and my baby daughter, Rachel, and share lunch with them. What a precious season: I was in the middle of a new family and a new ministry ... exciting and overwhelming at the same time!

It was also a season where I was beginning to step out and write songs, something I wasn't sure I was qualified to do, but something I felt God inviting me into. The writing of songs goes nowhere without inspiration, that initial spark that gets the song rolling. Sometimes the spark appears in the middle of normal, everyday activities; other times it comes at unusual moments and in unusual locations. And when it comes, it can sometimes be like a faint whisper that I can hear only when I am really still; other times the inspiration comes so strongly it's almost audible. The idea for "Refiner's Fire" came in the middle of a normal day, but the inspiration was anything but routine, and the place where I received it seemed like a peculiar place to start writing a song.

Returning to the office after lunch, I pulled up to a traffic light at the corner of Fraser Highway and the #10 Langley Bypass, which is a major intersection. While I waited for the traffic light to change, I was suddenly aware of a holy presence. I thought that just to my left, outside the car window, I heard a phrase being sung over and over: "Purify my heart, let me be as gold …" It would fade away for a moment and then start again, just repeating those two phrases. I say "heard" because I don't know how else to describe it. It sounded audible to me, but I doubt that anyone else in the cars around me heard anything but the noise of traffic. It was one of those rare times when I felt the presence of God so strongly that I heard something. And it wasn't just in my ears—I felt something too. There was power like electrical current coursing through my body. I was having a God encounter at a traffic light on my lunch break! Eventually[2] the light did turn, and I continued driving back to the office, singing that line over and over so it wouldn't slip away.

When I arrived back at the office, I asked my secretary to hold all calls so I could hide away with my guitar, Bible, and concordance in the back corner of the old furniture warehouse where our church met. I started by singing that phrase over and over again: "Purify my heart." I spent time in prayer, asking God to do that very thing with me. And then I began asking the question behind the phrase: "What makes us pure?"

One of the pictures that started to emerge was the picture of the bride of Christ getting herself ready for the wedding day … desiring nothing but purity.

I meditated on passages like 2 Corinthians 7:1: "Since we have these promises, dear friends, let us purify ourselves from everything that contaminates body and spirit, perfecting holiness out of reverence for God."

One of the great promises of God that we are waiting for is intimate union with Him—all of us together, the redeemed from every tribe and tongue who will make up the bride of Christ. It's because we are looking forward to something so wonderful and pure that we can say no to things that may feel good in the moment but will pull us away from faithfulness to God. Keeping our hearts fixed on the beauty of the Lord can prevent us from straying. I often wonder if David wrote Psalm 27 before or after his sin with Bathsheba:

> One thing I ask of the LORD, this is what I seek: that I may dwell in the house of the LORD all the days of my life, to gaze upon the beauty of the LORD and to seek him in his temple.
> (v. 4)

Writing Psalm 27 before facing temptation could have helped prevent what followed. Or maybe David wrote it after the fact, affirming that only gazing on the beauty of the Lord will protect him and lead him into life. My hunch is that he wrote it before—but he forgot it … and chose not to live it out. Interestingly, in his sin with Bathsheba, David got into trouble not just because his eyes were wandering—he got into trouble because he didn't go to war.

> In the spring, *at the time when kings go off to war,* David sent Joab out with the king's men and the whole Israelite army. They destroyed the Ammonites and besieged Rabbah. *But David remained in Jerusalem.* (2 Sam. 11:1)

There are some strong parallels in our lives.

The best defense against temptation is always a strong offense. The best way to "affair proof" your marriage is to have an ongoing romantic affair with your spouse, pouring all your love and energy into having a great marriage. Joyce and I have a date night almost every week, and several times a year we go away for romantic getaways. Tragically there are so many flings even in the church— romantic and sexual encounters that tear covenantal relationships apart. God designed us to experience the thrill of a romantic sexual encounter; the rekindling of passion with our marriage partners.[3] It just takes some planning and prioritizing. (I've heard that having an affair takes lots of planning and secrecy—why not spend that energy on surprising your marriage partner?)

For many of us, especially men, our eyes are never satisfied. This constant hunger was a key factor in David's story. A multibillion-dollar industry uses the modern technologies of still and moving cameras, print, cable, and the Internet to degrade and dehumanize women—and is built around the sad truth of our fallenness: "Death and Destruction are never satisfied, and neither are the eyes of man" (Prov. 27:20).

Death and destruction—two scary companions and comparisons for the eyes of man!

Oh, that God would purify our hearts so that our eyes would stop wandering! The primary issue isn't with women's clothes (or lack of them!). The primary issue is with our hearts.[4]

And the best way to squash the feelings of uselessness that can lead to seeking out distraction and entertainment is to be actively engaged in the battle over people's hearts and in the worship of our King.

"Refiner's Fire" has been very important to me when I struggle with temptation.[5] I find this song on my lips often, and it helps bring me back to my deepest desire: to be set apart for God. We spend lots of time focused on lesser desires when our greatest desire is for union with God. We need to keep stirring up the "one desire" in our hearts.

Lots of people say that the key to purity is suppressing our desire for pleasure. Remember when hair shirts and self-flagellation were "in" with the God-seeking crowd? I don't believe that smothering our desire for pleasure is the answer at all—or ever. Here is what C. S. Lewis had to say in his essay "The Weight of Glory":

> *If there lurks in most modern minds the notion that to desire our own good and earnestly to hope for the enjoyment of it is a bad thing, I submit that this notion has crept in from Kant and the Stoics and is no part of the Christian faith. Indeed, if we consider the unblushing promises of reward and the staggering nature of the rewards promised in*

the Gospels, it would seem that our Lord finds our desires not too strong, but too weak. We are half-hearted creatures, fooling about with drink and sex and ambition when infinite joy is offered us, like an ignorant child who wants to go on making mud pies in a slum because he cannot imagine what is meant by the offer of a holiday at the sea. We are far too easily pleased.[6]

The goal of purity is not for us to be purged from all of our bodily and physical desires. Our bodies are gifts from God and need to be seen as good!

Listen to C. S. Lewis on how God sees our bodily desires:

I know some muddle-headed Christians have talked as if Christianity thought that sex, or the body, or pleasure, were bad in themselves. But they were wrong. Christianity is almost the only one of the great religions which thoroughly approves of the body—which believes that matter is good, that God himself once took on a human body, and that some kind of body is going to be given us even in Heaven and is going to be an essential part of our happiness, our beauty and our energy.[7]

The key to purity is in eagerly desiring the greatest pleasure of all: knowing God. That's what I meant in "Come, Now Is the Time to

Worship" when I wrote, "Still the greatest treasure remains for those."
The greatest treasure is the pleasure of knowing God intimately, not
simply heaven in some distant and merely theological sense.

And in order for us to immerse ourselves in this life of knowing
God, we need to set ourselves apart for God. The verse that prob-
ably influenced the emerging song the most that summer day was 2
Timothy 2:20–21:

> In a large house there are articles not only of gold and
> silver, but also of wood and clay; some are for noble
> purposes and some for ignoble. If a man cleanses himself
> from the latter, he will be an instrument for noble pur-
> poses, made holy, useful to the Master and prepared to do
> any good work.

We play an active role in setting ourselves apart. The phrase
"cleanses himself from the latter" jumped out at me. It is as we do our
part that we are made holy and prepared for what God has for us.

The reason I chose to use the word *Master*[8] in the song because
it's used in this passage. Even though that word doesn't sound relational to our modern ears, it speaks of a willing surrender of our lives
to God, which leads to relationship. Out of a deep desire to please
God, we are "prepared to do any good work." That's why I ended the
song with the phrase "ready to do Your will." That's where purity of
heart and being set apart land us: in a place of readiness.

Almost all of our heroes from the Scriptures were set apart in
some way for God. Some of them made radical choices, led by the
Spirit to do so. Others were set apart by God Himself.

Think about Samuel

His story starts in the bizarre period of history when a man could have more than one wife. In this case, Elkanah had two—talk about a recipe for contention and comparison! One of his wives, Peninnah, had many children, but Hannah, his other wife, had none. Peninnah would goad and provoke Hannah until she would weep and could not eat … while Elkanah would pour out extra affection on Hannah and provide her with a double portion of food. This is one of those rare descriptions in the Old Testament of a man's deep devotion to and affection for his wife. Hannah would regularly go up to the house of the Lord to pray … and ask for a son! She made a vow in the presence of the Lord: "O LORD Almighty, if you will only look upon your servant's misery and remember me … and give [me] a son, then I will give him to the LORD for all the days of his life, and no razor will ever be used on his head" (1 Sam. 1:11).

Isn't that interesting? She is desperate for a son, but she is willing to give him up. Oh, the inexplicable and baffling depths of the heart of a mother! I'm not sure we husbands and fathers will ever fully understand what goes on in their hearts. Of course, if you know God like Hannah or Abraham did, you know that giving up your child to God will lead to life and good things (with some suffering along the way).

We know the rest of the story. Eli the priest watches her in distress, thinking she is drunk, and he tries to send her away. But upon finding out the truth, he sends her out with a blessing. And God remembers her—she is soon with child. After she weans little Samuel, she returns to Eli at the temple and hands him over! Samuel's whole life is set apart for serving the Lord. And it's out of those years of being set apart that Samuel learns not only to voice his prayers, but also to listen to the voice of God. I'm sure that Samuel didn't realize at the beginning that he was being trained to speak God's word to the whole nation. All he knew … was that his mother had set him apart for God. And I'm sure at a certain point, that choice became fully his own. It had to become his, for all around him (even in the temple) was wickedness. The description of Eli's sons is dreadful. The things they did, even in the temple, were horrible! But Samuel was set apart for God, and he kept himself pure. I'm sure his mother's intercession had something to do with it. And for sure, it was vitally important that Samuel himself daily choose to keep his heart reserved for God.

Think about Samson

The story of Samson also begins with a couple longing for a son. This time God appears through an angel to Manoah's wife. The angel announces that their coming son is to be a Nazirite (which comes from the Hebrew word that means "separated"), and he will begin the deliverance of God's people from the Philistines. Samson is born as the direct fulfillment of this prophecy. Once he becomes a man, his story takes many bizarre turns. Samson desires a Philistine wife— which is a really bad idea in that culture and time—but God put that bad idea in Samson's heart because He intended to provoke a fight with the Philistines, who were ruling over Israel.

Reading epic stories like this reminds me that God has unique purposes for certain people. It's so easy to critique and analyze from a distance, but God alone knows our hearts and knows that unique reason we have been created.

And sometimes conflict and the breaking away from establishment are a "God" thing, even though most of us always see conflict as a bad thing. There are times when God simply says, "Enough!" That doesn't mean that a particular government, organization, or person is gone over night. But it does mean that certain organizations, nations, and people can move beyond redemption. Remember what God said about Eli's sons?

> Eli, who was very old, heard about everything his sons were doing to all Israel and how they slept with the women who served at the entrance to the Tent of Meeting. So he said to them, "Why do you do such things? I hear from all the people about these wicked deeds of yours. No, my sons; it is not a good report that I hear spreading among the LORD's people. If a man sins against another man, God may mediate for him; but if a man sins against the LORD, who will intercede for him?" His sons, however, did not listen to their father's rebuke, *for it was the LORD's will to put them to death.*
>
> And the boy Samuel continued to grow in stature and in favor with the Lord and with men. (1 Sam. 2:22–26)

If that story wasn't right there in our Bibles, I'm not sure we would believe it! The Lord decided that Eli's sons would have to go. So sometime later the Philistine army took care of that for God. In 1 Samuel 4:10–11 it simply says:

So the Philistines fought, and the Israelites were defeated and every man fled to his tent. The slaughter was very great; Israel lost thirty thousand foot soldiers. The ark of God was captured, and Eli's two sons, Hophni and Phinehas, died.

Corruption and impurity in the house of God lead to judgment on a nation.

But if we, who are called to minister to the Lord, keep our hearts pure and focused on God, we not only release blessing for our lives—we can bless a nation! We just need to know that as we seek to be set apart for God, we will likely be surrounded by other people who are actively doing the opposite. We give ourselves over completely to God and to doing His will in the midst of many who are giving themselves over to depravity.

Thankfully we don't need to pronounce the judgment of God. We just need to seek God, and He will take care of it in His time and way!

Think about Paul

He was on a mission from God (at least that's what he thought!) to stamp out the followers of the Way. He thought, in his human religious wisdom, that the followers of the Way were weakening and tearing apart the Jewish way and faith. But instead of allowing Paul to continue to arrest the Jesus followers, God arrested him on the Damascus road. God kept him in a dungeon of darkness for three days—he couldn't see and did not eat or drink anything. I wonder if he thought that his life was over.

Later on, when he writes to the Galatians, Paul describes this period of time when God set him apart:

> I want you to know, brothers, that the gospel I preached is not something that man made up. I did not receive it from any man, nor was I taught it; rather, I received it by revelation from Jesus Christ.
>
> For you have heard of my previous way of life in Judaism, how intensely I persecuted the church of God and tried to destroy it. I was advancing in Judaism beyond many Jews of my own age and was extremely zealous for the traditions of my fathers. *But when God, who set me apart from birth and called me by his grace,* was pleased to reveal his Son in me so that I might preach him among the Gentiles, I did not consult any man, nor did I go up to Jerusalem to see those who were apostles before I was, but I went immediately into Arabia and later returned to Damascus.
>
> Then after three years, I went up to Jerusalem to get acquainted with Peter and stayed with him fifteen days. (Gal. 1:11–18)

Paul was set apart by God … and then set apart from men for a period of time before he began his ministry. As a result, his ministry was not built upon human authority, but on God and His purposes.

What are we set apart for? What does it mean to be ready to do the will of God?

We are set apart to know and love God. Our highest calling is to love God and to do His will. And being ready to do the will of God means being ready to go to war. The idea of going to war was initially a struggle for me … and honestly it still is! I was raised a pacifist (Mennonite Brethren, an Anabaptist denomination), and so my family disdained any talk of war, viewing it as unnecessary on the AD side of the cross. What I didn't realize was that the way the world wages war and the ways of the kingdom of God are radically different—and that difference was true on the BC side of the cross as well!

The world's warriors are chosen for their skills, cunning, and strength—for their ability to stand tall and proud and fight well. God's warriors are chosen based on purity of heart: the humility of bowing down in worship and choosing complete submission to their Commander in Chief. Strength feels like the best choice for victory in war, but in God's kingdom, only purity leads to victory. It makes no sense in human terms that purity of heart would either qualify or disqualify you as a warrior. But that's the way it works in the kingdom of God.

This is powerfully illustrated in the story in Judges 7 when Israel starts out with a vast army of 32,000 soldiers to defeat the Midianite army. The Lord bluntly says to Gideon, "You have too many men…. In order *that Israel may not boast* against me *that her own strength has saved her*, announce now to the people, 'Anyone who trembles with fear may now turn back and leave Mount Gilead'" (Judg. 7:2–3).

Obviously God was not pleased when Israel relied on her own strength, and I believe that God has not changed His view in the era of grace this side of the cross.[9]

In Gideon's story God whittles the army down from thirty-two thousand to three hundred. That is crazy—and it gets even crazier! How's this for a battle-winning strategy: Instead of sharpened swords, hold lanterns covered by jars in one hand and a trumpet in another, and on cue smash the jars and blow the trumpets. And God does the rest!

That's it! That's God's crazy plan!

The warriors don't get to demonstrate their swordsmanship or their courageous skill in battle. This time they get to demonstrate their trust and submission to their leader and watch God win the battle for them. And that's saying nothing about the humiliating way the three hundred were picked in the first place. It's not like there was a big contest of strength and the three hundred strongest were chosen. Isn't that the way we would have done it? We would have devised something like "Survivor: The Warriors Challenge"—something that showcases strength and agility. And we wouldn't have whittled down the numbers in the first place. We are completely convinced in the modern world that bigger is better—strength in numbers will win the day.

Luke records a baffling story in Luke 9: Jesus sending out the Twelve on a ministry trip with some strange instructions. He forbids them to bring any supplies. No suitcase, no money, nothing. Why would He send them out with nothing?

I believe He wanted them to turn away completely from relying on human resources to accomplish God's work. And it worked. They lacked nothing. God supplied their every physical need as they supplied the spiritual needs of those they ministered to.

And just when you think that's the rule for every ministry trip until the return of Jesus, we read this later on in Luke 22:

Jesus asked them, "When I sent you without purse, bag or sandals, did you lack anything?"

"Nothing," they answered.

He said to them, "But now if you have a purse, take it, and also a bag; and if you don't have a sword, sell your cloak and buy one." (vv. 35–36)

The principle of not relying on human resource remains. But His specific instructions were different each time they went out … which means that they are unique for us as well!

The Scriptures state it so bluntly: "God opposes the proud but gives grace to the humble" (James 4:6).[10] God is not looking for man's strength—not even our gifting and talents. (Ouch! This hits pretty close to home to us creative musician types!) God is looking for purity. God is looking for our hearts. He will use our gifting and talents in the kingdom, but *only* if they are first tempered through the refining fire of God's holiness, only if we can lay down our gifts at His feet. He tells us when we are to pick them up again, if ever. Many times as a worship pastor, I am amazed at how quickly new people will announce their giftedness to me or other pastors, as if their ability on their instrument is the sole determining factor in getting on the stage and leading God's people in worship.

Worship is not about bringing our best talents to try to impress God with a performance of our strength. That's how the world wages war. Worship begins with what we are willing to surrender to God.[11]

This is one of the things I observe when I go out to consult churches in their worship music ministries. People believe that what they bring

God (their performance of songs, etc.) is the core of their worship. And if I suggest to them that they should lay it down, they may feel like I'm saying they should stop being worshippers. That's not what I am saying. The core of our worship is not found in what we do for God, but rather in what we are willing not to do—what we are willing to surrender. That's one of the reasons that I encourage all worship team members to "resign" once a year. Lay it down and see if God and those around you confirm that you should pick it up again. It could very well be that some of your most powerful worship offerings (from heaven's perspective) are the times when you are not playing or singing on a stage.

There are many other amazing stories in the Scriptures that illustrate this principle of walking in surrender and obedience. How about facing a city God wants you to win in battle—and your only battle strategy involves walking around the city in complete quietness for the first six days? Everything within us wants to do something smart or strong that will win the day. God says, "No, thanks ... today I want to use your silence." I heard Kevin Peat, a wonderful preacher from Scotland, recently say that sometimes God commands us to be quiet so we don't talk ourselves out of a miracle. I can relate to that! Sometimes we just need to trust God, shut up, and get on with obeying His battle plan. Sometimes God likes to offend our minds in order to reveal our hearts. And why is God so concerned about revealing our hearts? Because it's the condition of our heart that is of paramount importance in the kingdom of God.

That condition is one of the key differences between Saul and David.

Saul was a man of impressive strength and stature; David obviously wasn't ... he wasn't even considered by his family to be a possibility when Samuel came with the horn of oil to anoint the next king. But God called David "a man after his own heart" (1 Sam. 13:14). Wow! That's some affirmation! Isn't it interesting that what God affirmed had to do with David's heart? Of course, David was not perfect. (Don't you love that about the Scriptures as well? They don't hide or gloss over all David's sins and faults.) But David was a man who was going after God's heart. He was always pursuing. He was always asking for forgiveness. He was crying out to God: "Create in me a pure heart, O God" (Ps. 51:10).

The desire for purity before God that burned in David's heart is another amazing contrast between Saul and David: Saul tries to justify himself when he is caught in disobedience; David is the king of transparency. When David is caught in sin, he goes into deep repentance and mourning—he does not try to justify himself!

If we don't understand the pure heart principle in the kingdom of God, we will exhaust ourselves trying to help God along. We will offer only our strengths while hiding our weaknesses and failures. But our best plans will be thwarted—because God isn't looking for our strength. He is looking for purity of heart.

So that's why singing words like "Purify my heart" is so danger-ous … and so important. It prepares us to see God. It prepares us for battle. Our calling and role in God's unfolding redemption depend on our hearts being purified. And our relationship with God depends on it as well.

Being ready to do the will of God doesn't just mean entering the spiritual war by doing something mystical or symbolic in a charismatic church service. It means being ready to love your spouse and provide for your children. It means doing everything practical to serve and love people—for the God we worship loves the whole world and longs for none of them to die in their sins!

We are set apart to do the will of God.

Matthew 5:8 says, "Blessed are the pure in heart, for they will see God." This is the heart of worship—to see and know God. Surrendering to the process of purity. And it's this kind of worship that the Enemy actively opposes. A choice to be a worshipper means a choice to be thrust into the battle of the kingdom of God. But if we keep our hearts pure, we can hear from God in the midst of the battle.

The 2 Timothy passage we looked at earlier shifts us from the battlefield to the kitchen, but the heart of the meaning is still the same.

> In a well-furnished kitchen there are not only crystal goblets and silver platters, but waste cans and compost buckets— some containers used to serve fine meals, others to take out the garbage. Become the kind of container God can use to present any and every kind of gift to his guests for their blessing. (2 Tim. 2:20–21 MSG)

The New International Version says, "If a man cleanses himself …" and The Message phrases it, "Become the kind of container …" However you word it, the choice we make determines how and where God will use us.

That's the choice I have made. I'm spending my life crying out to God for the gift of purity and making every choice within my power to set myself apart for the very thing I have prayed for.

Is that the same desire burning in your heart?

SONGWRITING TIPS

Be ready for inspiration whenever and wherever it comes. The key is to recognize it when it comes—drop everything you are doing, and attend to the inspiration until you have truly captured the essence of it and can recall it to keep on refining it.

Stay on track saying one thing. It's quite easy as a songwriter to get carried away and start saying all kinds of things. Songs are designed to say one thing, and you need to focus on that one thing.

Include expressions of repentance and dependence in your songs. We have bought into our culture's way of thinking, believing that God wants to use only our strengths—so we should hide away our weaknesses. A song is a perfect place to confess who we really are!

Anchor your song in Scripture, even if the finished lyric is distinctly different from the Scripture that inspired the idea. In this song I used words and concepts from several Scriptures. You can tell that it is rooted in Scripture even though it's not a literal Scripture song.

Notes

1. Brian Doerksen, "Refiner's Fire," © 1990 Vineyard Songs Canada and ION Publishing. Used by permission.

2. It seemed like time was frozen while this was happening, so it felt like I was having this experience for some time.

3. Of course, a marriage relationship isn't all about the passion and the thrill. It's about faithfully serving each other and finding ways to build each other up. But good romance is about that, too! As someone once said, "The best sex in the bedroom starts by helping in the kitchen."

4. I *would* like to make a pitch for modesty in women's clothes—especially in worship ministry! Women can help men by not drawing our eyes.

5. Okay, I don't mean to spoil your perfect image of me, but I struggle with many of the same things you do. My thought life is not always perfectly pure! And if I were to defend and define myself with my own moral righteousness, it would amount to a hill of beans (and probably one that you would be allergic to!).

6. C. S. Lewis, *The Weight of Glory* (New York: HarperOne, 2001).

7. C. S. Lewis, *Mere Christianity* (New York: HarperCollins, 2001), 98.

8. On several occasions I have substituted the word *Husband* for *Master* because that's what the cry of the bride of Christ is about.

9. "When I first took over the defense of the Gospel, I remembered what Doctor Staupitz said to me. 'I like it well,' he said, 'that the doctrine which you proclaim *gives glory to God alone and none to man.* For never can too much glory, goodness, and mercy be ascribed unto God.' These words of the worthy Doctor comforted and confirmed me. The Gospel is true because it deprives men of all glory, wisdom, and righteousness and turns over all honor to the Creator alone. It is safer to attribute too much glory unto God than unto man" (Martin Luther, *Commentary on Galatians 1:11, 12,* [Whitefish, MT: Kessinger Publishing, 2004], 27).

10. See also 1 Peter 5:5 and Proverbs 3:34.

11. This is another wonderful thing that handicapped and disabled children and adults show us: The most important things to God are our hearts and the ability to receive and give love. My wife and I would have never signed up to have handicapped children, but our boys with fragile X syndrome have brought this revelation home right into the heart of our family and right into the heart of the worship songs that I write.

Fortress 144

You are my God
You are my fortress
My loving God
My refuge and shield

You are my God
You are my stronghold
Delivering me
From the father of lies

Part Your heavens and come down
Touch the mountains so they burn with fire
Send forth lightning from on high
Scatter all who would oppose Your light

All praise to You my rock
Who trains my han'ds for war!
All praise to You my rock
Who trains my hands for war![1]

CHAPTER 5

Fortress 144

Have you ever seen pictures from war zones where civilians are trying to live a normal life while battles rage all around them?

Who would intentionally choose to live in a battle zone? I know I wouldn't. Yet the truth is we're all born in a war zone, and we all spend our days in occupied territory! We are in the middle of an ancient war, yet most of the time we try to live as if it isn't so.

This is a tough song for me to sing.[2]

Maybe that's a strange thing to admit, since I wrote it. I was born to Mennonite parents.[3] I grew up in a conservative country church: East Aldergrove Mennonite Brethren in the Fraser Valley, where my dad led the hymns most Sundays. Though it's not the only distinctive characteristic, pacifism is one of the key marks of what it means to be a Mennonite.[4]

So for me, singing about being trained for war is a real stretch! But God has called us to something bigger than our cultural and family roots—and following that call often means the comforts of our home denomination need to yield to the reality of the kingdom.

Here's a truth that I never heard growing up in the church: *Our survival depends on learning the ways of warfare.*

Growing up, my survival seemed to depend more on making sure that I didn't drink alcohol, dance, or smoke. My calling was not about being on the offensive but being on the defensive—at least that is how it appeared to me when so much attention was given to the "thou shalt not" rules.

And in this context, when something terrible or tragic happened, it was simply part of the mysterious sovereign will of God.

It couldn't possibly be that this terrible thing—a brutal crime committed or a disaster befalling some unsuspecting people—was a result of the battle between good and evil. No one ever considered or mentioned the thought of someone being a casualty of war.

I am so grateful for my heritage and the many good things about my upbringing. I was raised to love the Word of God. I was taught that faithfulness is important. I learned to sing the great hymns of our faith.

But there were certain aspects of the ways of God that were left out, certain truths that were left in the treasure chest. Perhaps the leaders thought them too dangerous to handle. But it was almost as if certain parts of the Scriptures didn't exist!

We need the full counsel of Scripture to live in this perilous world. We need all of Scripture … and we need to know how to apply it to our lives. Through Scripture and through all the gifts of the Holy Spirit, we can learn the art of hearing the voice of God.

I believe that the church is restoring the biblical warfare worldview. This is critical and right.

In a world at war our survival depends on staying in step with our Commander in Chief. He sees the lay of the land and knows where our Enemy is preparing an ambush against us. He greatly desires to see us through this war so we can share in His victory. In order to be effective in the war, we must learn the ways of warfare. We must learn to handle the weapons God gives us.

Here is something that I don't think many people consider as they get dressed in their Sunday best and drive in their nice cars to attend their local church: You are heading for boot camp. You are going to meet with your Commander to receive your marching orders.

The gathering of the church is meant to be a number of things: a hospital to heal the sick and wounded; a family where everyone is enfolded and accepted; a school where we are taught the Word of God so we can be prepared for life's challenges; an athletic race where we encourage one another to keep our eyes fixed on the prize; and an army that engages and defeats the Enemy to see the kingdom of God advance.

Becoming a worshipper means becoming a warrior.

And by toning that down—or cutting it out altogether—we have sent men and women away from the church in droves. It's time to call them back. We need the warriors to return.

But we need them to return as worshipping warriors. That doesn't mean that all we do is sit around and sing—but singing is very powerful when it is done in the might of the Holy Spirit. Singing can awaken our hearts and terrify our enemies with melodies of truth. We will sing on into eternity. Often the problem with singing is not the singing—it's the sitting around!

What I mean the most by the phrase "worshipping warriors" is warriors, male and female, who are surrendered to God. Warriors like David who know that their authority comes because they are under authority—warriors willing to wait (even when everyone around them is rushing ahead!) or act decisively, using force if necessary to walk in obedience.

Since the resurgent rise of radical Islam has directly affected the Western world, people view the mixing of warfare words with God talk as a Molotov cocktail—a very dangerous, unpopular, and incendiary combination. We try to do everything we can to tone down the militaristic language in the Scriptures and live non-confrontational lives. It's like our highest calling is to be nice! As though, if we would just go out and be sweet, the demon warriors of hell would see the folly of their rebellion and lay down their weapons.

Where do we get that from? Was Jesus always nice? Was Jesus always passive? Was He always tender and mild?

We've cut out, or in the least like to skip over, some of the difficult statements of Jesus—like this one:

> Do not suppose that I have come to bring peace to the earth.
> I did not come to bring peace, but a sword. (Matt. 10:34)

In the parallel passage in Luke 12:51, The Message renders Jesus' words like this:

> Do you think I came to smooth things over and make everything nice? Not so. I've come to disrupt and confront!

There's that *nice* word again! And the concept of "smooth[ing] things over" involves making things seem in better shape than they really are. Jesus is a truth teller; He wants us to hear the truth! He wants us to see clearly—to see things as they really are so we can change!

It seems to me like someone slipped us some rose-colored glasses so that we don't see things as they truly are. Let me say something about that expression. I wonder if the first person who used the phrase "rose-colored glasses" ever came anywhere near actually growing roses. If you grow roses, as I do, you know this is not an easy task—it's a battle. Roses are full of thorns, and so the beautiful blooms and fragrance from a rose come at a great price—often the blood and sweat of the gardener! And what color do you see when you look through those glasses? I am guessing they are inferring a pale shade of red ... but roses come in every color (except black!).

I actually think roses are a picture of a life of worship. Fragrant yet there are thorns. Beautiful yet raised in suffering.

Back to the battle.

This battle exists because there is a rebel who is leading the charge against YHWH and all the followers of the Lamb. The demon hordes of hell are not going to lay down their weapons because we are nice to them!

> Woe to the earth and the sea,
> because the devil has gone down to you!
> He is filled with fury,
> because he knows that his time is short. (Rev. 12:12)

The fury of the Enemy will not be averted or subdued by our nice programs or wishful thinking.

Revelation 12:11 describes an aspect of our part in this great battle:

> They overcame him
> by the blood of the Lamb
> and by the word of their testimony;
> they did not love their lives so much
> as to shrink from death.

We are called to be overcoming warriors! And we can be little *w* warriors because our King is a capital *W* Warrior!

He's a warrior, not because He loves to kill and destroy, but because He defends and protects His own. Our King is a warrior because there is a rebellion against His rule and reign.

There's a war going on. And from eternity past that war is over worship. Lucifer and a third of the angels didn't want to worship God; they declared open war through their rebellion. And that war has been brought down to planet Earth.

If we don't believe that, there will be many things that won't make sense.

Where is the sense in the stories of women being raped and killed for moments of twisted pleasure? How can you explain the tragedy of a whole family being wiped out by a drunk driver?

So many people, upon hearing of violent crimes and tragedies like this, lift their fist towards heaven and say, "If God is a God of love, why are so many terrible things happening?" I ask the opposite question: "The universe is in open rebellion against its Creator ... so why are so many good things happening?"

At the core of everything is freedom—wonderful because it leads to relationship ... terrible because it leads to heartbreak and tragedy.

Why does God give us this terrible and wonderful freedom? Because He knows that love and relationship are only possible because of freedom.

God will not give up freedom and force everyone to love Him. He continues to offer us the freedom of choice: to choose Him or not to choose Him. That freedom is part of what makes up the core of His being. And it's what makes us unique, made in His image.

The God we worship is the source of freedom ... holy freedom!

I remember the season when I wrote this song. It had been a hard year. Some things had not gone the way we had hoped. I wanted to see if the coming season could be easier and more relaxing. I went to the Lord in prayer and asked for some time off.

There was silence from heaven.

Can you just picture God sending one of His angels to Satan with a message like this? "Could we call a cease-fire? My followers have had all they can take, and they need some time off from the battle!"

Now I do believe there are times when God in His compassion hides us from the battle for a season. He gives us an extended Sabbath rest. But for me the coming days were not to be restful.

He directed me to the book of Nehemiah and instructed me to gather courage from his example. The fourth chapter gives this amazing description of the people's awareness of the battle they had to work with:

I stationed some of the people behind the lowest points of the wall at the exposed places, posting them *by families*, with their swords, spears and bows. After I looked things over, I stood up and said to the nobles, the officials and the rest of the people, "Don't be afraid of them. *Remember the Lord, who is great and awesome, and fight for your brothers, your sons and your daughters, your wives and your homes."*

When our enemies heard that we were aware of their plot and that God had frustrated it, we all returned to the wall, each to his own work.

From that day on, *half of my men did the work, while the other half were equipped with spears, shields, bows and armor.* The officers posted themselves behind all the people of Judah who were building the wall. Those who carried materials *did their work with one hand and held a weapon in the other,* and *each of the builders wore his sword at his side as he worked.* (Neh. 4:13–18)

Nehemiah could not deny the reality of the threat before them— it needed to be faced with a show of force. The Enemy waits for the walls of protection to crumble. And if that breach is not protected and built back up, the Enemy walks right through that opening with every intention to occupy.

I love the fact that Nehemiah posted people by families. What a powerful truth! This is one of the reasons that the Enemy has waged war against the family. If he can weaken and ultimately separate families, he can slip through the breach in the wall unchallenged. But it's not his territory—it's ours ... and ultimately God's, for "the earth is the Lord's and everything in it" (Ps. 24:1).

Really all we need to do is resist—for the power of God that is in us as we are submitted to the Father is enough to send the Enemy away. Satan is able to occupy only those places that we have given him access to. Listen to these powerful New Testament passages:

Resist the devil, and he will flee from you. (James 4:7)

Be self-controlled and alert. Your enemy the devil prowls around like a roaring lion looking for someone to devour. Resist him, standing firm in the faith, because you know that your brothers throughout the world are undergoing the same kind of sufferings.

And the God of all grace, who called you to his eternal glory in Christ, after you have suffered a little while, will himself restore you and make you strong, firm and steadfast. (1 Peter 5:8–10)

And so God stations us in places where there is need ... and places in our hands the weapons of war.

Each of us is commissioned by God to do specific things in the kingdom, but we all have to keep a sword by our side. The sword is the Word of God, the prayers we pray, and the way we spend our lives protecting the ones who are precious in His sight.

My cowriting partner on this song, Steve Mitchinson, has a real calling as a warrior. In the natural world he is a medical doctor from England now living in Canada ... but in the spiritual realm he is a mighty warrior in worship. Steve and I set out to put Psalm 144 to music in a fresh way—a way that conveys the urgency of our need to recognize the battle that we are in![5]

Actually, this song didn't begin on one of my songwriting retreats with Steve. It began the previous year, when I was in Kansas City at a conference in the fall of 2002. I was in a hotel in the center of the city—about fifteen floors up, looking over the city and praying.

I asked God this simple question: "Why are You gathering Your people?" And what I heard surprised me. I sensed God say, "I want to train them for war!"

So I headed to the Scriptures and found Psalm 144 … and I sensed in my spirit that the prayer of David was being renewed in our day. And I started singing what is now the chorus over and over again: "All praise to You my rock who trains my hands for war!"

David lived in an era of history when there was great struggle over protecting the lineage of the coming Messiah. From God's vantage point (and ours three thousand years later) everything that was happening was narrowing toward the fulcrum of human history—about a thousand years after David when the Messiah would be born to a Jewish teenager, fulfilling all of God's covenant promises! God did not want His covenant people intermarrying with the other nations … not because God doesn't have a heart for all nations, but because He was working His plan for the Savior to be born—a descendant of Abraham, Isaac, and Jacob. God is a covenant-making and covenant-keeping God, and if we don't understand this, we will misinterpret some of the stories in the Old Testament!

God knew that these other nations, with whom He had not made a covenant, would pull the heart of His people away from faithfulness to Him … and He knew that these nations were utterly given over to the worship of idols and wickedness. So God declared war on them. God decreed their destruction. And for God to declare war on a people means that they have fallen into depravity that is beyond redemption—a terrifying place to dwell!

So David, along with many other leaders of God's covenantal people in that era, was called to enter battle in God's name and destroy the enemy. In these battles God's people were affirmed for wiping out the enemy and rebuked if they left survivors, because those survivors would ensnare the Israelites into their brand of idolatry and depravity. It was a different world, but a necessary part of the unfolding revelation and plan of God toward redemption. And that was God's ultimate goal—reconciliation with His creation.

David's pride and joy didn't come from vanquishing many foes on the battlefield … his greatest joy was in being in the presence of God. Through it all David's heart was focused not on the enemy and not on his own fears, but on God.

The story of David's emergence and his first victory in battle over Goliath reveals his heart well:

> David said to the Philistine, "You come against me with sword and spear and javelin, but I come against you in the name of the LORD Almighty, the God of the armies of Israel, whom you have defied. This day the LORD will hand you over to me, and I'll strike you down and cut off your head. Today I will give the carcasses of the Philistine army to the birds of the air and the beasts of the earth, and the whole world will know that there is a God in Israel. All those

gathered here will know that it is not by sword or spear that the LORD saves; for the battle is the LORD's, and he will give all of you into our hands." (1 Sam. 17:45–47)

Those are fighting words!

And they are also words of worship.

There's a little something in what David says that is hugely important: "It is not by sword or spear that the Lord saves" (v. 47). Isn't that awesome? Even though David was trained to use the sword and praised God for training him, he knew that battles were not truly won by human strength. The battle is the Lord's! Yes—it was true on that day in the valley of Elah, and it is true today. The battles we are to fight are His battles, not our own!

As we embrace God's call to become worshipping warriors, we need to remember that we are not called to wage war as the world does: "For though we live in the world, we do not wage war as the world does" (2 Cor. 10:3).

When I sing the line from Psalm 144 about my hands being trained for war, I think about it this way: The Messiah was sent to Israel, and He lived a flawless life. He went to the cross to die and then by the power of God was resurrected. Now, instead of narrowing to the point of the Messiah's arrival, history is opening up in the other direction. Yeshua, the Jewish Messiah, is Jesus, the hope of all nations. The covenant is extended to every tribe and tongue. Grace and salvation are being offered to all. Jesus has struck a decisive blow to the Enemy, but the battle rages on—so now God wants to use my hands for acts of love that invite the presence of God and push back the darkness of the Enemy.

So as a worshipping warrior in our era, I don't use my hands for violence. I use them to protect and build up. I lift my hands in prayer and worship. I handle the Word of God and speak it out.

I do all of these things as a son and soldier in the kingdom of God.

Through my life and all my actions, as well as my prayers and my songs, I am demolishing strongholds set up against God.

> For though we live in the world, we do not wage war as the world does. The weapons we fight with are not the weapons of the world. On the contrary, they have divine power to demolish strongholds. We demolish arguments and every pretension that sets itself up against the knowledge of God, and we take captive every thought to make it obedient to Christ. (2 Cor. 10:3–5)

Our prisoners of war in the spiritual battle are no longer flesh-and-blood people—they are thoughts that pull us away from our devotion to Jesus.

And our armor and weaponry are given to us by God.

> A final word: Be strong in the Lord and in his mighty power. Put on all of God's armor so that you will be able to stand firm against all strategies of the devil. For we are not fighting against flesh-and-blood enemies, but against evil rulers and authorities of the unseen world, against mighty powers in this dark world, and against evil spirits in the heavenly places.
>
> Therefore, put on every piece of God's armor so you will be able to resist the enemy in the time of evil. Then

after the battle you will still be standing firm. Stand your ground, putting on the belt of truth and the body armor of God's righteousness. For shoes, put on the peace that comes from the Good News so that you will be fully prepared. In addition to all of these, hold up the shield of faith to stop the fiery arrows of the devil. Put on salvation as your helmet, and take the sword of the Spirit, which is the word of God.

Pray in the Spirit at all times and on every occasion. Stay alert and be persistent in your prayers for all believers everywhere. (Eph. 6:10–18 NLT)

We are no longer fighting against flesh-and-blood enemies like David did—no, we are duking it out with demons. Actually David had the joy of fighting against both human forces and spiritual forces; we just fight the latter.

Of course, we can still be attacked and harassed by our flesh-and-blood enemies, but our calling is not to retaliate against people. God does put the sword in the hand of earthly governments to restrain evil, and I am very grateful for the work that police officers and those enlisted in the military do to protect and defend our nations.

But as worshippers, our primary battle involves contending with spiritual forces.

I remember leading worship in Halifax some years ago. As I prepared and prayed, I sensed there would be some sort of showdown that morning. And as I led worship, God's presence came and exposed a demonic spirit dwelling in someone who was attending the service. The spirit within the person started screaming out; some people immediately gathered around and restrained the person. We commanded the spirit to leave, and it did! Confronting evil spirits is not something to be frightened of; it's just something that we need to do. We have authority over demonic spirits when we are walking with Jesus.

I don't think we should go around looking for demons, but I do think that we should be living in such a way that we are ticking off demons. That's certainly what we see in the life of Jesus!

The Ephesians passage also brings in the concept of resisting. We are called to resist the Enemy in the time of evil. Putting on God's armor is what enables us to resist. The Enemy is shooting at us. Fiery arrows are constantly headed our way. Thoughts of discouragement. False accusation. Demonic desires that are not our own, masquerading as though they come from us.

Guess who has been speaking and stirring up these things?

The father of lies!

This is the battle we are in—and it's a life-and-death battle.

That's why singing songs of worship filled with truth is so important! Songs go into our spirits, hearts, and minds and move us to action. And songs help us remember.

Studies have been done about the human brain, memory, and music, and they learned that music goes into a special part of our brain that is different from reading prose, listening to speech, or reading the written word.[6] When a person cannot recall information, the special "musical" part of the brain can recall words that were set to melody. People who can remember almost nothing can still sing songs that they learned before they lost most of their short-term and even long-term memory.

I'm so grateful that I still have my memory—but life is fragile, and I don't know how many days I have left … so with every day God gives me, I am going to keep on sowing songs of worship into my mind and heart.

Songs of love and intimacy. Songs of war. All of them saturated with God's truth.

And with every chance I get to lead worship, I will continue to sing intimate songs of the Father's love, songs of love and gratitude to my Savior. But I also remember to use the songs that are written to help us wage war. There is a time for music to awaken the slumbering warriors. Now is that time.

SONGWRITING TIPS

Find fresh ways of singing the Psalms. I don't think the content of the Psalms will ever go out of style or become irrelevant. Granted, Psalm 144 is one of the tougher ones to set to music — but it's still needed.

Don't be afraid of the "out of key" chords. In this song, I use both the flat 6 major 7 and the flat 7 major (Cmaj7 is the flat 6 and D is the flat 7). If you have no idea what I just said, and your heart is being stirred to write music, taking a basic music theory course would be really helpful and actually lots of fun. Understanding the basics of how music works helps unlock all the potential building blocks of music so you can write songs that move other people.

Be patient with your song fragments. I wrote the end section first, and for six months I couldn't unlock the rest of the song until Steve helped me write it. Make sure you document well what you have so that you can return to it.

Take a risk lyrically, including things that are unexpected but true. I watched a few people raise their eyebrows the first time they heard the phrase "father of lies." But that is the battle we are in: a battle over our thoughts and coming into agreement with God.

Notes

1. "Fortress 144" by Brian Doerksen & Steve Mitchinson © 2004 Integrity's Hosanna! Music/ASCAP. Used by permission.

2. I would rather sing about peace. I would rather sing songs of comfort … and I do sing many of those songs because that is part of what God offers us!

3. The Doerksen family is Mennonite as far back as we can trace: the early 1800s in the Russian Mennonite colonies.

4. The beliefs and practices of all the pacifists and groups committed to nonviolence continue to accomplish much good in our world!

5. Beyond hearing my version of this song on *Today,* you should check out Steve's version, which he sings with Jeff Deyo on his powerful CD *War of Love.* It totally rocks! (www.ionworship.org)

6. I was listening to a radio program while driving when they talked about this— and because of my life in music, it stuck with me.

Today
(As for Me and My House)

Today I choose to follow You
Today I choose to give my "yes" to You
Today I choose to hear Your voice and live
Today I choose to follow You

As for me and my house
We will serve You
As for me and my house
We will spend our lives on You
Today!

Wonderful Counselor
Everlasting Father
Eternal King, Lord of Hosts
Willingly we follow
Today[1]

CHAPTER 6

Today (As for Me and My House)

If you are singing songs written in the twenty-first century, you won't find the word "today" in any top ten lists for words most utilized. But the word's lunar opposite is ubiquitous in the vocabulary of modern pop songs.

If you go to a lyric Web site and search for the word "tonight," you get a staggering number of songs. Next to the word "baby" (and that is not a reference to an infant!), "tonight" is one of the most used words in pop music.

But in the Scriptures, God keys in on "today." Here are just a few of God's hit verses:

> Come, let us bow down in worship, let us kneel before the LORD our Maker; for he is our God and we are the people of his pasture, the flock under his care. *Today,* if you hear his voice, do not harden your hearts."
> (Ps. 95:6–8)

See, I am setting before you *today* a blessing and a curse—
the blessing if you obey the commands of the LORD your
God that I am giving you *today;* the curse if you disobey the
commands of the LORD your God and turn from the way
that I command you *today* by following other gods, which
you have not known. (Deut. 11:26–28)

See, I set before you *today* life and prosperity, death and
destruction. For I command you *today* to love the LORD
your God, to walk in his ways, and to keep his commands,
decrees and laws; then you will live and increase, and the
LORD your God will bless you in the land you are entering
to possess.

But if your heart turns away and you are not obedient, and if you are drawn away to bow down to other gods
and worship them, I declare to you *this day* that you will
certainly be destroyed. You will not live long in the land you
are crossing the Jordan to enter and possess.

This day I call heaven and earth as witnesses against
you that I have set before you life and death, blessings and
curses. Now choose life, so that you and your children
may live and that you may love the LORD your God, listen
to his voice, and hold fast to him. For the LORD is your
life, and he will give you many years in the land he swore
to give to your fathers, Abraham, Isaac and Jacob. (Deut.
30:15–20)

Today salvation has come to this house. (Luke 19:9)

Do you hear a consistent theme in these verses?

God doesn't want us to wait until it's night to make our crucial decisions. He wants us to make them in the clear light of day. He wants us to know what we are doing.

This song started to take shape on New Year's Eve. In the Western world New Year's Eve and New Year's Day have become turning point days—a time of reflection on the past and a hopeful looking forward into the future.

As I was praying and consecrating myself and my family to God, I remembered a single phrase God had impressed upon me a few days earlier: *Today I choose to follow You.* And then I immediately remembered the story of Joshua, surrounded by people wavering in their choice to follow God.

Use your imagination to place yourself in the middle of that wavering, confused crowd. Listen to the words as Joshua's voice booms out over the Israelites on that day.

> Now fear the LORD and serve him with all faithfulness. Throw away the gods your forefathers worshiped beyond the River and in Egypt, and serve the LORD. But if serving the LORD seems undesirable to you, then choose for yourselves this day whom you will serve, whether the gods your forefathers served beyond the River, or the gods of the Amorites, in whose land you are living. But as for me and my household, we will serve the LORD. (Josh. 24:14–15)

Words filled with authority, passion, and freedom! I wonder what Joshua was feeling as he raised these words over the dusty, confused crowd? Was he feeling confident? Or was he trembling with fear? Whatever he was feeling, I'm sure he was being carried along by the strength and spirit of God. Joshua brought clarity to a people who were struggling with confusion, and he offered a clear choice to those who lacked conviction.

This wasn't anything new to Joshua. Remember when all the spies returned from Canaan? Ten of the twelve said, "There's no way we can do this." Joshua was one of the two who stood alone on that day—even when the people threatened to stone him—and said this:

> If the LORD is pleased with us, he will lead us into that land,
> a land flowing with milk and honey, and will give it to us.
> Only do not rebel against the LORD. And do not be afraid
> of the people of the land, because we will swallow them up.
> Their protection is gone, but the LORD is with us. Do not be
> afraid of them. (Num. 14:8–9)

The Lord is with us. Joshua knew it was all about staying faithful to YHWH; as long as the people stayed close to God and His heart, they would be protected and provided for.

So once more these people needed to decide their allegiance.

Joshua clearly holds out the truth: There is nothing as important as faithfulness. More than anything, God wants us to forsake other loves and masters and choose Him.

But He always gives us a choice.

The invitation always carries with it the possibility that we can decline and go our own way. There are other gods we can serve … there are other paths we can choose. Godly leaders in the church do the same—like Joshua, they decisively and clearly hold forth the invitation, but they release people to make their choice. It never works to make the choice for other people. Each of us must choose.

The words "seems undesirable" in Joshua 24:15 are loaded. The challenge is that often serving the Lord feels "undesirable." And herein lies one of the biggest challenges for leaders in the kingdom of God. The other gods and pagan philosophies have really good marketing campaigns. They are really good at enticing people with the promise of pleasure (and leaving out the real price or just putting it in the fine print of the contract!). So we need to hold out the whole picture—the whole truth of what's really at stake. We need to tell the stories of God's provision in our past just like Joshua did on that day. We need to give people leadership and clear vision for the future.

And we must know that there is no option to "pass" on this choice. It's impossible not to choose. You must make a choice.

Either you will serve the Lord or you will choose another master, even if in the most modern of choices you are serving and worshipping only yourself.

You can look back in your past to the gods your forefathers served[2] … or you can take your cues from the culture all around you ("the gods of the Amorites, in whose land you are living"—Joshua 24:15).

There will always be lots of options, lots of gods that want your devotion, service, and worship.

What should we do with those other gods?

On that day, Joshua's passionate counsel was that we throw them away! He shouts, "Throw away the gods your forefathers worshipped!"

This is a powerful picture—on one hand is this worthless god … and then there's YHWH! In this case some of the Israelites literally held a god that they served in their past in one hand. On the other hand (but never in it!), they could serve YHWH, the Creator of the universe.

What's in your hand that you need to throw away?

I can guarantee that it's worthless next to who God is. But remember: I cannot choose for you. You must choose.

I realize that these things we hold in our hands are hard to let go of … and every culture and generation has them. They may not look like literal idols anymore, but they still have spiritual power because we have given them our devotion!

Joshua essentially said, "But as for me … I have chosen YHWH, and my family and I will serve God and His purposes in our generation." When Joshua made his choice, he was also choosing for his household. That's how it worked in that culture and period of history—the choice and word of the father was law.

In our modern world the fathers of our families don't have that much power. When men don't have good hearts and morals, it's a positive thing that they don't have that much power. But when men have good hearts and are following God, their decisive leadership is life giving and enabling for all those around them. How much greater would the blessings be for the women and children in our culture if the fathers and husbands began leading by example?

Husbands, fathers, it's time for us to serve God in such a way that our families are compelled to join us, just as we serve them and keep our hearts joined with theirs.

When I made my choice to serve the Lord and pour my heart into kingdom ministry of various types, I was choosing to bring my family with me into this life that God had ordained for us. But for me and my house, the choice of how to serve God hasn't always been clear and simple.

I decided that I would not sacrifice my family at the altar of ministry, because I believe that God does not delight in that type of sacrifice. There are sacrifices that bring joy to God's heart—this is not one of them! Yet this is actually one of my struggles with certain Scriptures and especially aspects of the New Testament where some of the key leaders (like Jesus and Paul) were single and I … well, I'm not! I live with the reality of a wife and six children.

For one thing, trying to do music ministry to the broader church often requires time away from home … but the price of my absence is very high with a large family that includes special-needs kids. I have an amazing wife, Joyce, who is incredibly resilient and multitalented (she is much more mechanical than I am). But she needs the intimacy and support that I alone can give as her husband. And as a sensitive and creative person, I need the rhythm of regular family life to keep me anchored and peaceful.

Yet as men, getting that invitation or opportunity to do what we are gifted to do is a very affirming thing. And that affirmation can become addictive and dangerous if our homes are not filled with affirmation that runs both ways between husband and wife.

And affirmation takes work and effort to sustain, because the years themselves can start to take a toll on both of you.

The years have taken a toll on my wife—no, not in that way! She looks as good or better almost twenty-five years after our marriage than she did on our wedding day. (I'm a completely different story!) The years have taken their toll in areas like physical weariness and being emotionally spent raising six children, including some with special needs. The years have taken their toll on me too, though for me it's evident physically with my shining brow (that's code for not much hair left) and a growing belly (that's plain and simple enough—I guess I could blame that on my wife's amazing cooking). It's also been tough emotionally and physically for me. Going through some intense conflict in the church and in ministry has decked me. The weight of the future—arranging care for my sons—sometimes gets to me. Changing diapers on our youngest child, who is now ten years old, wears both of us down. And I notice that it takes me a bit longer than before to recover from an international trip because of jet lag, etc.

But what continues to be clear and simple is that I want to stay faithful—to my wife, to my children, and to my God. Even though I am tired at times, there is nowhere I would rather be than with my family and worshipping my God. And if from time to time I do need to go out to teach and share the music that God has given me, I go out in the confidence that my family is right with me. Even if they are not with me physically for a week, they are with me in their hearts. And it's been awesome in the last few years to be able to bring one of my children with me on tours or to conferences. They help with practical things like product sales, and we just get some extra hang-out time together.

Serving the Lord involves living a life that pleases God … and it does little good to be gone so much that those whom God has given as our primary responsibility—our first neighbors—feel abandoned.

Jesus, in answering the question of the greatest commandment, says that loving God is so closely linked to loving those around us that they are inseparable. People have always tried to separate them.

"Love your neighbor as yourself." I believe that our first neighbors are our spouses and family members. This is life's greatest test!

We have special-needs children. And apparently over 80 percent of marriages with special-needs children end in divorce.

Joyce and I choose not to be part of that statistic. Even though aspects of our life are tough, God is with us. And so many days we look at each other and say, "We are the blessed ones!" For it's through our sons' needs that we are learning deeply about unconditional love.

In the midst of our life of caring for our children and doing ministry, Joyce and I choose to continue to build up our marriage. I take my wife on a date every week! For the last few years, Monday night has been date night. It's wonderful. Date night is a time to take a deep breath together and just be with each other. The activities vary … but the heart is the same.

To be with each other away from distractions.

To look each other in the eye and reaffirm our love for each other.

To have fun together.

To listen to each other.

To go for long walks together.

To plan together so that our lives complement each other and don't compete with each other.

And on top of our weekly evening date, she takes me out on several minidates during my workweek. Our current favorite spot is our local Starbucks, about a mile from our house, where we order tall soy chai lattes—180 degrees extra hot so we can savor them for a while, an extra pump so they're spicier, no water so they're not watery, and light foam so we don't lose a quarter of the drink to foam!

The point actually isn't the fancy drink—it's choosing to slow everything else down and stay connected in each other's worlds.[3]

For often it's on those latte breaks that we plan key ministry things together or get clarity on a key decision we need to make—or just have some time to talk about one of our children's current challenges and how we can help them grow into their next season.

We prioritize these dates and breaks because we know that most of life is not time spent sipping a latte—it's a battlefield.

And on the battlefield of life, it's critical for each of us to make this "Joshua choice" with each new "today" God brings us!

Today is the only day we have! Love God, and love your neighbor. They're both closer than you may think.

SONGWRITING TIPS

Focus your song around a key word. What is that word that jumps out at you, the one you sense you need to focus on? Build your song around that word!

Bring a little dissonance into your melody and chordal structure. That tension and dissonance reflect life all around us. If everything is too predictable, the song may be dismissed as too sweet. In the chorus of this song, I go from the V (five) chord to the II (two) minor, which is surprising. The melodic notes reach up to the fourth degree of the scale and back to the third, but over the II minor chord. That tension suggests that it's not easy for "me and my house" to serve the Lord. Someone tried to get me to eliminate this tension from the chorus—but I kept it because I'd put it there on purpose. Find ways to let these kinds of tensions tell a bigger story with your songs.

Don't let a song go by without bringing God and His character into focus. This song is primarily about declaring our choice to follow God. However, the bridge gives me a chance to lift up the character of the One we are following: Wonderful Counselor, Everlasting Father, etc.

Use a key change—not as a gimmick, but skillfully and artfully as a means to bring greater closing energy. In this case I composed the melody in such a way that the final note of the bridge became the first note of the final section in the new key, exactly one tone higher than where we started.

Notes

1. "Today (As for Me and My House)" by Brian Doerksen & Sandra Gage © 2003 Integrity's Hosanna! Music/ASCAP. Used by permission.

2. If your roots are filled with some kind of pagan worship or alliance with other gods, you must break those ties powerfully in prayer—or those bondages will reach out to ensnare you!

3. It's kind of like the Sabbath—you just plan in advance that one day in seven is given to rest and rejuvenation. And it's amazing how much better the other six days go when you give God that one day for you to breathe deeply and worship Him!

Psalm 13

(How Long O Lord)

How long O Lord will You forget me
How long O Lord
Will You look the other way

How long O Lord
Must I wrestle with my thoughts
And every day
Have such sorrow in my heart

Look on me and answer,
O God my Father
Bring light to my darkness
Before they see me fall

But I trust
In Your unfailing love
Yes my heart will rejoice
Still I sing of Your unfailing love
You have been good
You will be good to me[1]

CHAPTER 7

Psalm 13 (How Long O Lord)

It was a rainy night in February 2001.

We had traveled a long way to escape the rain—2,080 kilometers to be exact (that's 1,292 miles for my American friends!). Crammed into our Suburban, our family of eight from Abbotsford, British Columbia, headed south. Our good friends from England, Steve and Karen Mitchinson and their children, flew across the Atlantic Ocean to rendezvous with us in a place of warmth and sunshine. We only had about a week to spend in sunny Southern California ... and the weather was not being very kind to us. The rain would not let up. We hoped for a reprieve on the day we took the kids to Disneyland—but nothing doing. I'm sure you have heard the Disneyland marketing slogan: "The Happiest Place on Earth!" Whoever came up with that was not there on a cold, rainy day in February. There we were, lugging kids around in the pouring rain, thinking, "I spent how much to be cold and wet?" And then we got to spend more money on all those Mickey Mouse rain ponchos! Oh, what joy!

Then it was on to the beach the next day—and the rain seemed to kick up even more just to celebrate the arrival of the Canadian and British families laden with sand toys and beach towels. We looked longingly out of our motel window toward the beach … but we couldn't see the beach. All we saw was rain streaking the windows right in front of our faces, turning our view into tears of disappointment. Looking back, I wonder whether this song would have even been written if it weren't for that rain.[2]

At a point of exasperation my wife threw out a challenge to us: "Instead of complaining about the weather, why don't you guys do something useful … like write a song?" The challenge came with a deadline—Joyce and Karen were going out to Starbucks for coffee, and they wanted to hear a new song by the time they got back in a couple of hours! (I should state that this kind of challenge doesn't usually lead to a great song that stands the test of time.) As soon as they had walked out the door, we reached for our guitars, paper, and pen, dutiful and obedient husbands that we were. (I should add that, in the spirit of full disclosure, I am not always that prompt in my obedience.)

I recall saying to Steve, "It's a pretty good night to write a lament, don't you think?" Over the years I had wanted to write laments for theological and personal reasons, but it's never easy to do, and the timing just hadn't felt right. But this seemed to be the right time. I opened my Bible to the Psalms—God's treasure chest of laments—and found myself looking at Psalm 13. These words of David have always struck me as raw and painful, yet, like many of the psalms, tinged with hope in the middle of lament.

How many people can relate to feeling like God has forgotten them when they are in the middle of a painful time?

How many people have spent a night or two or ten wrestling with their thoughts?

How many have struggled with a heart weighed down with sorrow in the middle of a world that so often disappoints?

The number is too great to count.

And so, with the sound of dripping rain falling outside our motel room door to motivate us and help keep us in the right frame of mind, we started to write. My fingers fell to a B minor chord, and we began finding our melody for these timeless words of David. For the first few moments it didn't feel natural—it felt more like acting, probably because it hadn't been our idea.

But after about fifteen minutes Steve and I were immersed in the words and emotions of Psalm 13, and we could sense that this was the appointed moment to write this song. Any feelings of acting out the lyrics were long gone; we were living them as we sang.

And it was no longer about just the inconvenience and frustration over the rainy weather in sunny California. We were gathering up the many pains and sorrows experienced throughout our lives—and gathering up the disappointments of God's people as they wrestled with the realities of life in a fallen world.

The time flew by … and suddenly our wives were standing in front of us, rain dripping off their coats. Was it possible that two hours had already gone? We sang the song in its draft form, and even as we sang it to them, we could sense it was strong—we knew something powerful had just happened. Karen threw out a lyrical suggestion, and later Daphne, a friend who was singing on the recording, contributed a wonderful idea, adjusting some chords, which is why the women's names are on the songwriters' list. Maybe my wife's name should be on the list too, because she was the one who told us to write the song in the first place. And I have to admit, when she told us to write a song, I was not feeling inspired at all—it was the last thing I wanted to do. But I do know that I am called to give voice in song to expressions of intimate congregational worship, and sometimes as we step into what we know we are called to do, the feelings follow.

In the years since that rainy night, I have received so many encouraging letters and emails from people who identified with what we wrote. The reality is that the people who connected with the song the most are the ones who suffered in some way.[3] Some have gone through the unthinkable and inexpressible pain of losing their spouse to death or—even more heart wrenching—losing their spouse to unfaithfulness. For some it's the arrival of a handicapped child; for others it's the pain they received in the midst of a betrayal in the church. Whatever the source of the pain, when I lead worship I am always consciously reaching out for those who are quietly suffering in the back corner, not even sure they want to be at a gathering of worship. I want those people to have a voice because I know that God welcomes them into His house; He is waiting for them to bring their hearts, just as they are, into His presence.

Where else are we going to find real comfort?

In a bar?

In the arms of a stranger?

We as the modern church have done a poor job of welcoming the suffering and grieving into our community and gatherings. The sad truth is most of them don't even try to come because coming would just make them feel worse. Our worship services filled with exclusively happy-clappy songs feel totally out of touch with their suffering.

The modern worship culture of the megachurch makes it much easier to sing the big, shiny, happy anthems. But that culture of happy appearances and upbeat performances is keeping some brokenhearted people away from churches of all sizes.

> The sacrifices of God are a broken spirit;
> a broken and contrite heart,
> O God, you will not despise. (Ps. 51:17)

For the sake of the lost and hurting world, we need to sing songs of lament in our gatherings. For the sake of those who are already suffering, we need to include songs of brokenness. But writing those songs is not easy—and neither is even singing them—especially when the most common directive some pastors give to their worship leaders is, "More upbeat, joyful songs, please!" In other words, most often pastors and leaders have asked for the current, almost exclusive emphasis on big, shiny, and happy worship.

And for us writers, we know that writing any song (at least a good one!) is never easy—but it does seem easier to write the polished and positive anthems. So we give them what they want … but part of our hearts lies buried and hidden.

Maybe it's just easier to deny our pain. Singing pleasant and happy songs is less costly than being transparent and sharing our struggles.

David wrote all types of songs. Songs of trust. Songs of joy. Songs of grief and lament. But I can't say that any of David's songs were shiny or polished. He was not into the gleam of show or appearance. He was consumed by the reality of his humanity, and out of that honesty, he worshipped God with abandon!

I want to have the courage to be like Dave.

I want to bring all of my humanity and emotions into the house of God, just like Dave did. I want to worship God in every key, just like Dave did.

David seemed to be very clear on something that we have somehow lost through the centuries: God can handle all our emotions.

We can bring them all into God's house. What God can't handle[4] is when we ignore Him, when we pull out of relationship with Him. God hates when we hide from Him! It breaks His heart.

God hates being forgotten; He hates being ignored. That's not because God is insecure. No, it grieves Him because He knows that He is the source of all life and that it's only in relationship with Him that our lives will flourish!

Worship offered by humans has always included lament. And these laments will continue until God wraps up human history. If some preacher tells you that he has discovered the secret to ending all your suffering now … he's selling something. There are two clues to help you discern the false teachers, who are trying to take advantage of us as God's people.

First, they will use the language of "secrets." There's nothing new under the sun. Paul addressed the emerging heresy of Gnosticism in his letter to the Colossians; one of its keys was secret knowledge. Paul lets them (and us!) know that Jesus is the mystery of God now revealed. It's open—you don't need secret knowledge to know God and His ways. Jesus came to make it plain to all of us.

The second clue is a focus on "ending all your suffering now." Release from suffering is a promise beyond what Jesus Himself gave. It's the idea that we can return to Eden and live in utopia or nirvana now. But that marketing slogan usually comes with a common catch: You have to buy their products and do what they tell you to do!

Jesus said in John 16:33, "In this world you will have trouble. But take heart! I have overcome the world." Lots of religious spin doctors have tried to turn "you will have trouble" into "you had troubles." They promise that now that we are following the Jesus way, all our troubles will be over. That sounds like the promises made in modern pop songs! They usually go something like this: "Now that we're together, all our troubles are over."

Jesus says that trouble is unavoidable in this life. It's been part of our past, and it will be part of our future. That's not our fault. We can't banish all our troubles with some perfect declaration. Because we live in a fallen world, we suffer—all of us, even those of us who believe in Jesus. But as we go through trouble, and even though we will have trouble today and tomorrow, we can take heart; we can have hope, because Jesus has overcome the world. The victory is already won. It's a little like the timeline of the final year of World War II. D-day has come—the enemy is mortally wounded, and the outcome of the war is no longer in question.[5] But we are not yet at V-day, when the enemy finally surrenders!

Now, here on planet Earth, there are still battles being fought. There will still be suffering and casualties until the conclusion of this war that began in the heavenlies!

As we worship in the midst of a suffering world, we lament— not because we have no hope, but because we do. To bring lament is not to bring complaint as an end in itself; it's to bring our brokenness and grief to God and ask for His comfort and deliverance. Craig Broyles, a professor at Trinity Western University in Langley,

British Columbia, said this about the lament psalms: "The petition motif indicates that these psalms seek change and that they are based ultimately on promise, not doubt. They acknowledge that something is wrong and affirm God can put it right."[6]

Yes, this is true! God can make it right. As a worshipper I am trusting in the promise of God's good character. That's why I can come with who I really am into God's presence to express my humanity. And He welcomes all of us to do just that, to pour out our hearts in His presence.

Coming into God's presence is the way He intends us to deal with suffering and loss. Sadly so many people—even leaders in the church—have not taken up the biblical way to deal with loss. They follow the world's pattern, dealing with loss through denial and distraction.

We have all done it. Pretending we are okay. Denying that our hearts are broken. Filling our lives with entertainment.

Anything to divert our attention from how we are really doing.

For millennia God's people dealt with their pain and suffering by running into the house of God and pouring out their anguish to the One who was waiting for them. Yet in recent years taking anguish to God's house has fallen out of favor. If you want favor with church leaders and movements, make sure you keep the laments and songs of suffering hidden in some closet far away from our gatherings. Just keep on singing the shiny anthems, speaking the optimistic messages—and everyone will love you for it!

A few summers ago I sat riveted as Kevin Peat, a wonderful and funny Scottish preacher, shared on Psalm 13 in Scotland. It was the first time I'd ever heard a leader preach on one of the biblical laments at a major Christian conference—and I have been to many Christian conferences. It was powerful! Kevin wove Psalm 13 together with his and Margaret's story of inability to have children for over twenty years. The medical professionals told them that there was nothing wrong with either of their reproductive systems. They were prayed for many times. They confessed every sin they could think of. Still no children! His message that night was about our response when God seems to say no or delays in answering our petition. What choices do we make when we feel forgotten by God? Their life speaks a powerful testimony. The Peats have poured themselves out on behalf of the church in Scotland, and they have many spiritual children! They still don't fully understand why they didn't get the natural children they prayed for, but they did not become bitter.

After the meeting we shared a meal with the leaders of the conference. And one of the other leaders confided in me that they were not sure about the message Kevin gave—it could give Scottish believers permission to not expect results from God.

Not expect results.

I have mulled over those words. We love results in our modern world. The whole system of business is built on results! But is that how we should see our relationship with God and His response to our prayers?

Sometimes I get deeply concerned about the vending machine God that we seem to have created. Is it possible that we made this "God" in our own consumerist image? You put in your request, and *voila* … out pops what you asked for. You need healing? Just pray and you will be healed![7] You need prosperity? Just put in a request, and out comes the wealth you ordered!

God does not guarantee results in our walk of faith. Have you read Hebrews 11 lately?

Each of us on a journey of faith may not receive all God has promised in this life. But there is something that God does promise, and it's a guarantee: "Never will I leave you; never will I forsake you" (Heb. 13:5).

If Kevin Peat had received exactly what he wanted and prayed for, maybe he would never have preached a message on Psalm 13. If Joyce and I had received exactly what we prayed for with our sixth child and were not given the immense blessing of a second special-needs son, maybe I wouldn't have written a version of Psalm 13 or included laments during worship. Sometimes we don't get what we ask for. Sometimes God's blessings come in disguise. This is reality. It was reality for all the men and women of faith who have gone before us, and it's reality in our lives.

So why are we afraid of biblical laments?

This fear of dealing with pain and loss in the biblical way is causing turmoil in our emotions, increasing our emotional dysfunction and addiction to performance. And without the release laments bring, we're becoming sick! People in the world look upon us with disdain—not over the offense of the cross but over our dishonesty and plastic smiles as we just "praise the Lord." It's not just our culture that's into denial—it's the church as well.

"How are you doing this morning?" When you walk into church and you are greeted with that question, what do you do? How do you answer that question?

Some have said that the Sunday morning hour of worship is still the most segregated hour in the nation. I wonder if it's not also one of the most dishonest. We tell each other that we are doing "good" when our hearts are breaking, and we fill the air with the things that we think God wants to hear ... and leave all the things that are really going on inside of us unspoken.

These unhealthy ways of dealing with pain and suffering lead us away from relationship, from each other, and from God. Denial and distraction lead to alienation and isolation while biblical laments lead to relationship with God and real relationship with others in community. What pulls us closer than sharing our struggles or confessing our sins to each other? Pretending we have no issues only pushes us apart.

Loss and disappointment are inevitable. Suffering will be our close companion. It's how we respond to the suffering that makes all the difference. If we learn to suffer well, if we learn to suffer God's way, it will make all the difference in our lives. We don't have to become familiar friends with denial and distraction! Because we live in a fallen world—the result of an ancient war—and we struggle with our own fallen nature, we will face many valleys shadowed with death. We will want to back up and find a way around the valley or deny that the valley exists (one of the favorites of some "faith" teachers) ... but God's way is to go *through the valley* with His presence, comfort, and help!

David suffered greatly—at the hands of enemies, at the hands of his own family—and what did he do? He ran to God's house and poured out his response in prayer to God ... and because of that, he remained truly human!

David was feeling forgotten as he walked through one of his darkest valleys shadowed with death. When he looked up to see

God, all he could see was that God was looking away from him. And so David raised his anguish to the heavens with these words:

LOOK!!!

ANSWER!!!

If you don't look and see my plight—if you don't come to me and answer me, I will fall ... I will die![8]

For many centuries the core songs sung by the people of God were the Psalms. And what was great about this practice is the Psalms are like a well-balanced diet, containing all the important elements of what it means to be a human being in relationship with God in the midst of a fallen world!

The Psalms are sung prayers to God; sung prayers asking for deliverance and help; sung prayers of lament as people struggle with loss and hang on to hope! I have heard people say that anywhere from 20 percent to 70 percent of the Psalms are laments or contain an element of lament. Whatever number you pick, I believe we have a big problem in the modern Western church, because it's hard to find local churches including *any* laments in their modern worship repertoire!

And so this has been an area where I have taken a few steps to try to be like Dave ... and it's usually gotten me into some trouble with church and worship industry leaders. But what got me into trouble in the back rooms of religion helped me connect with hurting people!

Aren't you glad that the painful stuff and mistakes were not edited out of the Bible?

What do we do when we hear tragic news—especially the kind of tragic news that involves the moral failure of one of our leaders in the church?

Do we lament?

I tried that years ago when a major leader in our movement of churches fell, and I got soundly rebuked for even bringing it up—and doubly reprimanded for singing a lament. The church leaders wanted to ignore what happened completely and just carry on without him. I wrote a song called "One of the Warriors Has Fallen," inspired by the lament that David wrote when Saul and Jonathan fell in battle. David was crushed by Jonathan's death, but David also laments Saul, God's anointed, who just so happened to be trying to kill him. Instead of quickly moving on and trying to wipe out all references to Saul, David did one of the most courageous things a leader could do! He wrote a lament in their honor and taught it to the Israelites so that they could process what happened and express their grief instead of suppressing it.

We live in a culture that has reports of tragic news from around the world every day—but very few laments! Have you ever asked yourself whether we should be inundating ourselves with bad news that we can do nothing about? I believe that God wants us to be aware, but does being aware outside of our sphere of influence bring us life?

Maybe we should not be willing to hear news that we are not willing to lament and act on. If we don't lament and act, part of our humanity dies, and we become callous and hard. Were the words *callous* and *hard* ever used to describe David? They just don't go with David. Following after God's heart will always lead us into compassion and tenderness.

There are some teachers and worship leaders who would have us believe that we should not bring our sorrow, pain, and suffering into God's presence. They believe that the only thing appropriate for God's house are songs of joy and thanksgiving. I have sometimes wondered whether they have read the whole Bible! Yes, of course we need to bring to God our joyful thanksgiving; He is the source of every good gift! But He also longs to for us to feel safe enough and to trust Him enough to bring our pain, doubts, and laments to Him.

Let me give you a practical example. I am a father with six children. Each of my children is precious to me and deeply loved. When do you think I want to see them or hear from them? Only when they are doing great? Only when they do well on a test at school? I'll tell you when I most want to see them. It's when they are struggling and confused or when someone has mistreated them and they need comfort. How much more does our Father in heaven want to hear from each of us when we are struggling? He doesn't want us to wait until we sort ourselves out; He wants us to come right away and get comforted in His presence.

That makes me realize—*maybe the laments in Scripture were God's favorites!*

Laments arose during the times when His children came to Him in trouble. And what a testimony that is! Or is our relationship with God the type that we only show up when everything is going great? I vividly remember a moment from one of the plays I saw in London while we were living there in the late 1990s. The play was called *An Inspector Calls*. A young man is in deep trouble over some convoluted personal problems, and when his father eventually finds out, he comes to him and asks, "Why didn't you come to me for help?" The son's response riveted me and told so much about his father and their relationship: "Because you're not the kind of father that one can come to in trouble!"

Is God the type of father that we can come to when we are in trouble? If the answer is *no,* we are in more than trouble! But the wonderful truth of Scripture is that God is one who welcomes us when we need Him most!

I sometimes wonder whether the God who is worshipped in all the success-based churches and ministries is simply the Performance God that matches all our striving for attention and addiction to entertainment. When we are freed from orphan living and thinking and encounter God as Father, we no longer need to perform for approval, and we no longer need to live for entertainment. We, as secure sons and daughters, can be about our Father's business, because we are loved just as we are!

So why are there so many laments in the Psalms and so few used in our expressions of worship today? Do we have the same Father? Are we worshipping the same God? Was life totally different for David and the other psalmists? And why did the church use the Psalter as its hymnbook for centuries, and we now have abandoned singing the Psalms? Was it because people suffered in other generations but don't suffer in ours?

I found this interview with an internationally known worship leader and songwriter in a worship magazine somewhat telling:

> *Interviewer: Many of your songs speak of the joy of the Christian life, and though the Bible reflects this aspect of praise, what about the other side of*

the coin? How do we translate a worship song for people to praise God even though they are in the midst of terrible suffering?

Worship Leader: All I can tell you is I get a lot of letters from people who are suffering. And these people are tested so much more than we are, but they're so faithful. They don't want to be reminded of their suffering. And they've already prayed, "God, how long must we suffer?" But now they want to sing a song of praise because there's power in it.

If this leader is talking solely about persecuted believers, the answer makes sense to me. But I don't think that's the case, because the leader lives in a free and prosperous nation. But if the question is more, "I notice you tend toward songs of celebration and joy—where are the songs for the suffering?" then the answer is woefully inadequate.

Now I totally agree that there is power in praise, and there are many times when in the midst of suffering we simply need to see God again and praise who He is. But praise needs to rise from the ground of honesty—starting where we are, not starting where we think God wants us to be. That's the key difference.

Flattery is filling the air with what we think God wants to hear—what we think will get us God's favor. And there are warnings about that very thing in Scripture.

> They would flatter him with their mouths,
> lying to him with their tongues;

their hearts were not loyal to him,

they were not faithful to his covenant.

(Ps. 78:36–37)

I believe that flattery is at the heart of all false worship. It's all about manipulation instead of surrender. The worship of YHWH is about surrender. Idol worship has the appearance of surrender, but at its heart, it's all about getting favors from the gods. Doesn't that sound a little like expecting results from God? The focus is on the results, not on the surrender!

The things the Israelites said weren't necessarily bad. They said things that were true and good. But what they said with their mouths was not an indication of where their hearts really were. Their hearts were far from the God who had made a covenant with them.

In our era it's similar. It's not that the shiny, happy songs are saying bad or untrue things—but we need to think about what we are emphasizing and where our hearts are. Are we telling the truth? Are we living the songs we are singing? If all we ever sing or hear in our churches are expressions of happiness, we can easily slip into flattery as a habitual part of our worship expression.

Like so many things in the life of worship, it comes down to the heart!

God is much more interested in our honest expression than He is in our songs of pretense. Sometimes our greatest act of worship is just hanging on to God in the middle of the storms of trouble that threaten to engulf us.

And sometimes those storms are not outside us—they are in our heads!

Like David, most people struggle with sorrowful, dark thoughts at times. For a long time this struggle was one of the "unmentionables" in the church. If you struggled with depression, you became invisible and untouchable. David isn't talking about struggling with an enemy—a person or force outside of himself—in Psalm 13 (there are plenty of those psalms!). This time, his struggle is with himself, with his own thoughts. I have those days sometimes. I have a somewhat melancholy personality. I have never been diagnosed with depression, but I know good people who have. And for any of us who struggle with dark thoughts, it's so healthy to be able to express them to God. David's prayer is candidly directed to God. He expresses it all—dark thoughts, dark feelings—and reaches a climax on the word *but!*

But ... I trust.

Despite all the ways I feel forgotten, I will trust in Your unfailing love. In the face of the winds of adversity that whisper that I am abandoned, I will hang on to Your faithfulness.

The expression of trust is one of the ways in which a biblical lament is slightly different from singing the blues. Our songs from the Psalms don't end in anguish; we emerge with a "but" and a "still."

"Still I sing." We sing in the valley shadowed with death. Our songs endure not so much because of the greatness of the music or the words. They endure because they are anchored by our hope in God Himself. His love will never fail.

"You have been good." I can look back and recall moments and seasons in my life where You have carried me through.

"You will be good." And just like I can recall Your goodness from the past, I know that You will be good again.

Even to someone flawed and broken like me.

SONGWRITING TIPS

Pick one of the lament psalms, and set it to a new melody.
Even if you don't write it for the public to hear, it will do your soul
good to enter the world of the psalmist and make it your own!

Try building a song around a "minor" starting point. It seems
like almost all modern worship songs are built around major
chords; we need more songs that are built upon the honesty and
sadness of the minor chords.

Use a strong word to hinge or change direction. We used the
word *look* in the pre-chorus because it has an insistence to it, and
the words *but* and *still* turn the whole song in the chorus. What
word can you use to hinge or change gears in your song?

**Use the secondary dominant to surprise in your chord pro-
gression.** The dominant is the V (five) chord, which has a strong
tendency to resolve to the root (I) chord. In this song the root is
actually the VI—the six minor chord. The in-key III (three) chord
would be an F-sharp minor chord—but by making it an F-sharp
major chord, I created the secondary dominant. You can target
any "home" chord with a secondary dominant before it.

Write your own lament. Express some of your grief and loss. If
you have nothing to lament, maybe you are not risking enough
for love.

Notes

1. "Psalm 13 (How Long O Lord)" by Brian Doerksen, Daphne Rademaker, Steve Mitchinson, Karen Mitchinson © 2002 Integrity's Hosanna! Music/ASCAP.

2. Of course, it's all relative, based on geography—those several days of rain in desert regions of the world may induce a celebration and the writing of songs of joy!

3. And what is so encouraging about these letters and about what people share with me at my concerts is that in the secret place years ago, God made it clear to me that I am called to lead worship for the suffering.

4. Of course, I don't mean this in a theological sense—God can handle anything. But He will not abide our ignoring Him!

5. D-day was June 6, 1944, the day the Allies landed on the beaches of Normandy. By taking and keeping that strategic beachhead, the Allies ensured that the Nazis would lose the war. V-E day came almost a year later on May 8, 1945.

6. Craig Broyles, "Psalms of Lament," *Dictionary of the Old Testament: Wisdom, Poetry & Writings,* ed. Tremper Longman III and Peter Enns (Downers Grove, IL: InterVarsity Press, 2008), 384–99.

7. Some say healing is guaranteed because Jesus never turned away anyone who came to Him for healing. It's true that Jesus did many healings (and is still healing today!). But there are examples of people who were not healed—for example, only one by the pool was healed. And Jesus was God's Son walking the earth. That gives Him a little advantage over us as far as healing goes!

8. This is my own interpretation of the psalm.

Your Faithfulness

I don't know what this day will bring
will it be disappointing
or filled with longed for things
I don't know what tomorrow holds
Still I know I can trust Your faithfulness

I don't know if these clouds mean rain
If they do, will they pour down blessing or pain
I don't know what the future holds
Still I know I can trust Your faithfulness

Certain as the rivers reach the sea
certain as the sunrise in the east
I can rest in Your faithfulness

Surer than a mother's tender love
surer than the stars still shine above
I can rest in Your faithfulness

I don't know how or when I'll die
Will it be a thief
or will I have a chance to say good-bye
I don't know how much time is left
But in the end I will know Your faithfulness

When darkness overwhelms my soul
When thoughts are storms of doubt
Still I trust You are always faithful, always faithful[1]

CHAPTER 8

Your Faithfulness

Life is crazy sometimes … well, maybe most of the time. It's full of moments that don't go our way. It's full of things utterly beyond our control. For the few moments of ecstatic joy we get to bask in, there are many more that threaten to crush us with the weight of disappointment and confusion. Yet threading through all of life is something certain, something absolutely sure: the faithfulness of God, the only safe harbor from the storms of doubt and disappointment.

This is the story behind the song "Your Faithfulness," but it's also the story that surrounds our lives—an ongoing discovery that the blessings of God often come in disguise.

It was 1999, on a warm, late-spring day in London, England. The world was starting to go mad with Y2K dread. I was dealing with fear too … but while the world was focused on "Y," I was dealing with "X."

I was wrestling with the possibility that our sixth child might be born with a disability. I was grappling with whether God had stepped in sixteen hours after our child was conceived (almost nine months beforehand) to stop the X chromosome in our child from mutating.[2] About three years earlier, shortly after the birth of our twin girls (numbers four and five in our family), we found out what was causing the extreme development delays in our son, Benjamin, who was five years old at the time. After extensive testing, the doctor told us, "He has 'fragile X syndrome.' Daughters, just like your wife, can have it too, but because a female has two X chromosomes, the healthy X masks most of the negative effects of the mutated X."

And so we began a journey with an uninvited close companion!

If you don't have a clue what "fragile X" is, you are in the majority, just like we were before that day. Even though most people don't know it by name, it's the most common inherited cause of mental impairment (Down syndrome is the most common, but it is not genetically inherited). This impairment can range from learning disabilities to more severe cognitive or intellectual disabilities. Sometimes referred to as mental retardation, fragile X is the most common known cause of autism or autistic behaviors.

When Joyce and I walked down on the aisle on that November 1984 day, we didn't stop on our way out of the church to sign up to have special-needs children. We had a loving desire to have children; even before we were married, we talked of our desire to have a large family … a dozen children even! Oh, the joys of naive innocence and youth!

Shortly after moving to England with our five children in early 1997, in the wake of a devastating disappointment with the musical we were trying to launch, I felt God stirring my heart. It was time for another step of faith. But this step of faith was not a big ministry or music project. It was something much closer to home.

I sensed God inviting us to have another child.

In fact I specifically felt like God wanted to give us another son, one who would not be affected by fragile X syndrome. I shared this with Joyce, and she was experiencing similar stirrings. For months we talked and wrestled in prayer—*Was this God or just our own idea?* We didn't want to try to be heroes in our own strength! We didn't know how we would respond if faced with another devastating disappointment. We were just starting to recover, just starting to pull our heads above water, and we didn't want to go under again because it might be too much.

Let me share something from my heart that I almost never hear from Christian leaders. In moments like this, it's actually very difficult to clearly hear and know God's voice. If people tell you that it's always easy to hear God's voice, then maybe they have not been through devastating disappointments. Or maybe they have yet to experience what many call the "dark night of the soul." And then again, maybe they are just better at hearing God's voice than I am. It's hard to say.

So we decided to take the risk and try for another child. We were immediately faced with an incredible scheduling dilemma. We already knew that we were moving back to Canada at the end of July 1999; Joyce figured out that in order for her to recover from the birth before we had to move, the perfect and only time for this child to be born would be in early June 1999 ... which meant the child would have to be conceived in September 1998.

There was only one little problem. Of all the months of that year, September was the one where I was to be gone the most: to Europe for my first tour of worship concerts; to Ireland for a conference; for all the ministry kickoff activities of the new church year that corresponded with the school year. We could see it would take a miracle even to conceive. Add to the schedule this: Joyce and I have always been attracted to each other physically (always a good thing if you are married!), but this month was different. There was no spark between us … only stress! It's almost as if everything was conspiring against us having another child.

So when Joyce told me in October that she had conceived in September, my jaw dropped! How did it happen? Okay, I know how it happened (this ain't no virgin birth story), but how *did* it happen? After recovering from my surprise, I stepped into a surge of faith. If God gave us the gift of another child in the midst of all of this, I just knew that something very special was planned for this child—that he would be the son we were praying for. And so for the next eight months, I just knew! I knew what was going to happen. I knew that God had heard the desires of our hearts and all the prayers of our close friends and intercessors and pastors. I walked to work, as you do in London, with a spring in my step. I was going to be a father again, and this time I was going to have a healthy son, and we would talk about God stuff like theology and worship and the history of the world. Maybe he would learn to play a musical instrument, and we would make music together. Maybe we would sing together the same way I was able to sing with my father.[3]

I just knew that my Father in heaven was going to give us a son unaffected by fragile X. Joyce had a waking vision one day at an airport, where she saw me walking with two sons and knew the second son's name. In response to this vision, we planned to give him the name *Isaiah,* which has several meanings, including "God is generous."

I knew … until the final weeks of May 1999.

Spring had started to blossom in the beautiful English gardens outside … but on the inside, I entered winter as doubts blew into my mind like an unwelcome storm. Restless nights filled with dreams of children with severe disabilities and our inability to cope. Daytime hours filled with dread and a churning stomach.

I went through the motions of doing my job as a worship pastor. I walked my kids to school and did errands in town, but with each step I felt more and more overcome by the uncertainty of it all—and if you saw me walking to work, you would have noticed that the spring was gone from my steps. I started to cut myself off from people. A couple of days before the due date, I could no longer silently contain my struggle. I walked over to the piano … and soon the words and tears started to flow into a melody.

The first phrase out of my mouth was a confession: "I don't know." There was such release in saying, "I don't know! I don't know how this is all going to turn out."

"I don't know" doesn't mean I don't know what God is like; it means I don't know whether we heard right or whether things on this fallen earth will turn out the way we hope they will.

I don't know!

And as hard as it was to say those words, they also brought some freedom—because knowing sometimes comes with holding it all together and being in control … and God is asking us to yield control and trust.

In this moment I wasn't thinking about writing a song or reaching out to other people. I was just trying to survive the day! In my early days of church leadership, I thought I knew quite a few things.

Yet in that moment I realized I didn't know much. And I certainly did not know exactly what was happening in my wife's womb with the child she was carrying. All I knew was that our precious family was about to welcome another addition. And we were praying for another son, one who would not be affected by fragile X.

I began the "what ifs?" What if it was a girl[4] … what if it was a girl with Down syndrome? What if it was a girl with another type of disability? What if it was a boy—another boy with fragile X? If I was disappointed with any of these results of our step of faith, what would that say about my heart?

As the questions grew and fear threatened to overwhelm and mute me, I realized the faithfulness of God was the only thing I could count on—and can ever count on as I journey through life in a fallen world.

And so I began pouring out my heart into a melody that expressed both my fear and my faith. As I was honest with my fears, God made His presence known to me and filled me with trust—not that everything was guaranteed to work out the way that I wanted, but that He would faithfully remain with us every step of our journey. I likened this experience to stepping under some clouds filled with rain. Would the heavens open up and pour down blessings … or would they rain down pain and wash away our dreams of having a son who would carry on our family name? I know that we are often tempted not to take any risks, but as a wise preacher once said, "The only totally risk-free place on earth is the grave."[5]

And so, as I write this now in my home, I hear my son Isaiah crying and making moaning noises in the background. He's now reached the end of his first decade, and he has yet to speak his first words, other than "Noooooo" and "Mama." He's still not toilet trained ... though we are working on it!

Isaiah has fragile X syndrome.

The first year of Isaiah's life seemed completely normal (as it usually does with fragile X). We were simply basking in the goodness of God, and I spent many hours holding Isaiah, rocking him to sleep and singing over him a lullaby that I written for him.

Isaiah, Isaiah Robert
Isaiah, Isaiah Robert
In the autumn of 98
You were conceived by faith, Isaiah
Then in late spring of 99
You arrived on British time, Isaiah
And the meaning of your name
God is generous, Shining Fame!
Isaiah, Isaiah Robert
Isaiah, Isaiah Robert my son!

Then on a warm British Columbia summer day in 2000, we got the test results back: Isaiah was full-mutation fragile X. I stumbled around on our property for a couple of hours weeping ... confused, heartbroken, and feeling incredibly guilty that I was confused and heartbroken. At one point I lifted my voice to heaven and handed in my resignation: "God, I am through being a worship leader and songwriter who goes out and shares Your heart with the church. If after all the people praying for my son, and all our years of obedience, You can't come through and save my son from fragile X, then I am going to have to let go of my ministry dreams as well. I am going to simply keep my head down and provide, and maybe I can learn how to be a superdad for boys with fragile X—but I don't think I can do ministry and care for my family!"

My sense was that God was near, listening to my anguished prayer … but also listening to my pain-filled heart. Sometime later, when I was able to be quiet enough to hear, I sensed God holding out His hand and inviting me: "Will you still walk with Me? Will you still trust Me? Will you go on even with your broken heart and share My heart with My people—for who will relate to My people who are heartbroken if not those like you who are acquainted with disappointment?"

As I reflect on this now, I realize that I used to think people were most blessed by our great victories. But now I know differently: People are just longing to hear leaders speak of how they have walked through the deepest valleys and failures. The world lifts up the victorious and the successful, but God lifts up the brokenhearted!

Just recently I was on tour in Europe. When I told the story about our two boys after one of my concerts, a woman asked me in puzzlement, "If the doctors told you not to have any more children, why did you have another one?"

My simple answer is that I want God to have the last word.

I believe that children are always a blessing, even if they come with special needs and challenges. It was a risk we were willing to take—and to this day we have no regrets that we took that risk. We jumped, and the faithful arms of God caught us and hold us still.

That's all I really know.

SONGWRITING TIPS

A song is designed to say one thing. Keep on driving home the same message from different angles. In this song I confess what I don't know, what I can't control, all of which drive me back to utter dependency on God. This leads to another confession: There is only one thing I can count on—the faithfulness of God!

The more specific you become, the more universal the song becomes. I wrote this song out of the fear that my son would be born with a disability. I have received many letters of encouragement that this song has brought comfort to people in diverse situations. The circumstances are specific; the need is universal. We all need to come to trust in the faithfulness of God, because life doesn't turn out the way we planned.

Start each successive verse consistently. In this case I started each verse with the confession "I don't know ..." (I don't think I would have been so willing to confess that when I was younger; sometimes it takes some history and disappointments to knock the stuffing out of us!)

Embrace diversity in song form and structure. This song, while it may bear some resemblance to a standard verse-chorus song form, is actually written more in an AC form. Any of the A-based song forms (AAA, AABA, or AC) are different from a verse-chorus song in several key ways. A-based song forms come right out of the gate and give the key message of the song in the first section.

Often the key lyric of the song is found in the last line of the A section (as it is in the line "I can trust Your faithfulness"). The C in an AC form is sort of like a chorus, but it's different in that it's a release from the A to provide contrast. It may repeat the key concept of the song, but it doesn't introduce it, and musically it's not necessarily the high point or the point that you most remember. "Your Faithfulness" is an AC song with a bridge ("When darkness overwhelms my soul").

Use words to paint pictures. Word pictures help the listener remember the song. In the second verse I describe approaching clouds. I think we can all relate to this idea of knowing that sometimes the rain that falls is a blessing and that sometimes it's a plan wrecker.

Don't just declare your confident strengths—confess your humanity, your weaknesses, your fragility, and your questions. For some reason worship songwriting launches into this unending stream of confident declarations—but this confidence puts distance between the song and the lives of most people. Our songs should express who we really are, not who we think we ought to be. One is worship in truth; the other is flattery and religion. Of course there are times when we need to simply sing a song about the greatness of God. But worship needs to be a good balance of all of the human experience. That's why the Psalms worked so well; you find it all there!

Notes

1. "Your Faithfulness" by Brian Doerksen © 2002 Integrity's Hosanna! Music/ASCAP. Used by permission.

2. Fragile X research has determined that about sixteen hours after conception, part of the X chromosome shuts down.

3. My dad sang "It Is Well" with me on my CD *You Shine,* and when he can, he still sings with me at my concerts.

4. I should say that I have always completely delighted in each of my four girls; what treasures they are! But we took this step of faith not because we "needed" another girl, but because we sensed God wanted to give us another boy.

5. I believe Steve Nicholson, a Vineyard pastor in Chicago, said this, quoting another pastor.

Hallelujah (Your Love Is Amazing)

Hallelujah, Hallelujah
Hallelujah, Your love makes me sing
Hallelujah, Hallelujah
Hallelujah, Your love makes me sing

Your love is amazing, steady and unchanging
Your love is a mountain, firm beneath my feet
Your love is a mystery, how You gently lift me
When I am surrounded, Your love carries me

Your love is surprising, I can feel it rising
All the joy that's growing deep inside of me
Every time I see You, all Your goodness shines through
And I can feel this God song, rising up in me[1]

CHAPTER 9

Hallelujah (Your Love Is Amazing)

Why do the people of God sing?

Think about that for a moment. Singing is one of the peculiarly wonderful marks of the people of God around the world and throughout history.

Maybe in the modern age the question should be, "Why don't we sing anymore?" For the most part, people of the world have moved from singing to listening to other people sing for them. Think about how many viewers watch shows like *American Idol,* which is all built on evaluating and listening to other people sing. Our world loves to be entertained by singers, and I am astounded by how much fame and fortune we give people who can sing well.

The lost joy of singing is likely one of the downsides of the modern age of technology and electricity. In the past, if people wanted music, they actually had to gather around the piano and sing. Either they had to produce the music themselves, or they had to be physically present at a concert to hear the latest songs.

So for us as the family of God, singing is one of the things we need to cherish and continue to encourage as we gather. I have heard people criticize the modern worship movement—that instead of singing our songs of faith, our services and gatherings are becoming too much like rock concerts. As someone who enjoys and even plays rock music in the broadest sense of the term, I actually concur with that criticism at times. The attention can get way too focused on the band. The volume can get too high, to the point where you can't hear yourself sing.

One of the things we have done at our local church is meet in the round; the congregation faces each other in four sections like a diamond, and the band stands off to one end while the speaker is on the other end. The physical setup really helps underline that the gathering of our local church is not a concert. People gather to fellowship with each other and worship God. Being in the round actually helps people hear each other sing, and I encourage our sound team to keep the overall amplified sound at a medium level so people can still hear themselves and other people around them singing.

When I go out with my band to other places and do one of my worship concerts, I always try to have a good portion of the time where people are simply singing along with us. The sound is full (it needs to be to have energy!) but not overbearing. And usually the highlights of those events are when the band really dials down and we can clearly hear everyone singing a song that they love together.

Belonging to the family of God means that we belong to a singing family! That's what we do when we gather together!

We do it because we love singing—but most of all we do it because we love God, and it just seems like one of the most powerful ways to express it. And as we sing, we sense God's presence and pleasure.

He loves hearing His people sing.

The human ability to sing is actually part of what makes us distinctly unique in all of creation. We are designed with vocal chords that can be developed and trained to carry a tune. We can sing! What a gift!

At a recent worship conference we were having a roundtable discussion of new trends in worship, and people were describing all kinds of funky and creative ways to express their worship. They suggested a mixture of ancient things and new hybrids of creative expression. At one point I raised my hand and added my little contribution: "I can almost guarantee that in the future, one of the main ways we will express worship will be"—people leaned forward to hear the profound thing I was going to say (okay, that part was just in my imagination)—"in the future we will express worship by singing songs." There was silence … and then a kind of relieved sense of "Yes, that's right." In our quest to be trendy and creative, we can miss some of the most important things because they are so obvious!

God's people sing!

They always have, and they always will.

And what is it that makes us sing? What causes words to be lifted out of simple prose and speech and launched heavenward with melody? The sheer overflow of our hearts! Our songs spring from the intensity of emotion and conviction that cannot be contained.

I can still remember clearly the day when Brenton Brown and I started singing this song. Actually Brenton had started it on his own, and I helped him finish it in a surprising and funny way.

Brenton is originally from South Africa, and in the mid-1990s he moved to Oxford, England, to study at the university. I met him at a Vineyard event in 1997, and he became one of the emerging worship leaders I mentored while we lived in England. Around the beginning of 2000, shortly after we had moved back to Canada, Brenton came over for a visit to catch up with our family and to do some cowriting. On this particular day things were not going so well on the home front. Isaiah, our "Made in England" souvenir, was not a happy baby! My wife was in the kitchen, trying to make the family dinner, and Brenton and I were trying to be creative and write songs in my home office. Finally, in exasperation, Joyce brought crying Isaiah to me—put him in my arms and said, "You look after him for a while!" (Ironically, as I write these words, Joyce has left to run some errands, and I am looking after our now ten-year-old Isaiah in the very room where this story took place. Because of his special needs he can't be left unsupervised for too long.) So I headed to the living room to try to calm Isaiah down by sitting in the rocking chair. I sat there with him for a while, but he was still crying and still very fussy. A short while later Brenton burst into the living room with another idea. Now, being the clue-less single that he was at this time, he didn't get the direct and indirect messages that our songwriting session was over for the day! Isaiah was crying on my lap and not very impressed with the noisy singing going on, and I was looking at Brenton with a look that said *Perhaps now is not a good time* ... and he just launched into his idea anyway: "I have this idea for a song that I haven't played for you yet—I have a strong start to a verse, but I have no chorus ..." (All you songwriters out there can relate to this situation!)

And to my disbelief he started singing before I could tell him to shut it down: "'Your love is amazing, steady and unchanging. Your love is a mountain firm beneath my feet. Your love is a mystery—how You gently lift me—when I am surrounded, Your love carries me …' And that's all I have!"

And so with Isaiah squirming and fussing, I called out just to get Brenton off my case: "Why don't you do this for the chorus?"—and I sang out the melody literally as you know it—"Hallelujah … Hallelujah … Hallelujah … Your love makes me sing,"—and then sang it again!

Brenton looked at me and said, "No way!"—and I said, "Yes way!"

I immediately began to fight for the idea. I told him that I actually had been waiting for a fresh song where we just would sing the word "Hallelujah." It's such a rich God word, and I thought this would be a fresh, upbeat way to do it!

Well, I am still singing this song … and Brenton is too, along with other recording artists and worship leaders! It's been so fun to see the joy and celebration this song has released around the world—a very special gift for me, because my songs have tended to land more on the intense and intimate side.

What I intuitively did in that moment was I connected the God word with the concept of love in the verse—it's the love of God that causes these God words to burst forth!

And these words of worship that stir in us are such gifts.

Consider the word this song is built around—a wonderful, rich Hebrew "God" word—*hallelujah.*

Here's what it looks like in Hebrew:

הללו יה

The first part of the word—*hallelu*—means praise.[2] This form of *praise* is a plural imperative verb, and that's important, because that means that the worship leader is urging the community to praise—the song is not intended to remain an individual act of praise.

The ending of the word—the *jah* in English—is actually *Yah,* the shortened form of "Yahweh" or YHWH. This was God's personal and intimate name that revealed God's special covenant relationship with His people.

Most English versions of the Bible translate the first phrase of Psalm 111:1 as "Praise the Lord"; in Hebrew it's simply *hallelu Yah.* Eugene Peterson follows the original form in The Message. Note the connection to community.

> Hallelujah! I give thanks to GOD with everything I've got—
> Wherever good people gather, and in the congregation. (Ps. 111:1 MSG)

Now there are three meanings of this *hallelu* due to the three consonants—the "h-l-l." (In Hebrew only the consonants were written out.)

The most common use is to praise, to raise a cheer, to lift up a song of joy in adoration and admiration.

A less common but related use of the "h-l-l" is to shine or flash forth light. Isn't that an interesting thought? When we "Hallelujah," we are shining—reflecting the light of God back to Him, for He is light.

There is a third and rare use that has to do with infatuation, acting like a madman, boasting, and even looking foolish! We can remember the story of David dancing as the ark was brought back— I guess we could say that this was David doing the "Hallelujah."

In all of these meanings of *hallelu,* we recognize that this word is calling us to whole-minded, wholehearted, and whole-bodied praise. It's not a call to mere intellectual assent.

And one more thing about this word that's really interesting: The combination of *hallelu* and *Yah* is found only in the Psalms. It makes me think that we are meant to sing this wonderful God word. For the ancient followers of YHWH, when the phrase *hallelu Yah* was on their tongues, they were singing it! Perhaps God meant it to be set to music.

I think God gave *hallelu Yah* to us songwriters to inspire us to keep on finding fresh ways to sing the praises of God!

Now songwriting is not always as easy as it was for me that day. There have been a few "gift" moments like this where God seems to have taken the perspiration on Himself. But usually writing a song is hard work—like Thomas Edison once famously noted about success, it's usually 10 percent inspiration and 90 percent perspiration.

I am willing to do the work of a songwriter. The work of writing. The work of research. The work of rewriting and taking my time with a creative idea. The work of simply disciplining myself to show up for a writing appointment even when I feel nothing creative bubbling in me. I am willing to do all of these things and will continue to be willing for as long as God gives me breath. But I'm not going to turn down the gifts when they come. I'll just say thank you and know that the moment will not be repeated. More gifts will come, but no two of them are ever the same. And I'm still grateful for that gift in early 2000 when Isaiah was crying on my lap and Brenton was badgering me with his latest idea!

God loves hearing us sing. Especially when our songs are "God songs" … filled with God words and truths. But He longs for much more than that.

I remember a particular time when I was swept up by the power and beauty of a song. The song captivated me. The poetry, truth, and compelling melody drew me in. The arrangement was magnificent as well—the producer had chosen creative and interesting sounds to awaken my aural senses. As I was enjoying this musical moment, God questions popped into my head.

Is God enjoying this song the same way I am? Is the beauty of this singer's voice enough to bring delight to the heart of God?

Maybe we need to step back and ask a bigger question: Does God get delight from music? He must—He created it! Does God love creativity? How could a Creator not love our expressions of creativity? He delights in our songs … He loves all our expressions of creativity—*until* we are using those expressions of creativity to fake how we are really doing … *until* we are hiding behind our songs, even our songs of praise. A few fig leaves woven together, though creative and beautiful, were a sign that Adam and Eve were hiding who they really were from their Maker.

God does not need our music and our creative expressions of art to communicate truth or love. All of creation (even in a fallen state) does a pretty amazing job of that already!

> The heavens declare the glory of God; the skies proclaim the
> work of his hands. Day after day they pour forth speech;

night after night they display knowledge. There is no speech
or language where their voice is not heard. (Ps. 19:1–3)

So what does God need from us? What does He love to hear in
our music?

When we hear recorded music, our hearing is limited. We don't
hear the life of the musician or songwriter. And musically all the mistakes and out-of-tune notes have been edited out. Or to think about it
another way, we have started to see life through our culture's fascina-
tion with film and photography; now we often see only what's within
the frame. Outside of the frame and behind the facade and props built
for the film set or photo shoot, it's often not a pretty picture. For sure,
the stuff outside of the frame is not the part of the picture that we let
others see. But it's at this point that there is a big difference between
God and us.

We hear and see in part.

But God doesn't watch a film and see only what's in the frame.
He sees everything. There is nothing hidden from the eyes of God.

For the eyes of the LORD move to and fro throughout the
earth that He may strongly support those whose heart is
completely His. (2 Chron. 16:9 nasb)

What God wants to see is a heart and life completely devoted
to Him.

God doesn't listen to a song and hear only what the producer or
singer wants Him to hear.

He hears everything—everything we say and think.

God takes delight when the whole of our life, everything He hears and sees, is an expression of love to Him. If we are walking in unfaithfulness or lack of love, He is not impressed with our music, no matter how grand or beautiful it sounds to our ears.

Remember the warning in Amos?

> Away with the noise of your songs! I will not listen to the music of your harps. But let justice roll on like a river, righteousness like a never-failing stream! (Amos 5:23–24)

The issue is not the music—God loves music! Scripture contains way more commands to "sing a new song" than to "stop the music." The answer is not to shut down creativity; religion has tried that many times and failed. If you are anything like me, you have "God encounters" as you get creative! Our calling as musicians and singers is to love God with our whole lives—and flee our culture's proclivity to build facades that have no substance behind them. We live among a people that love to weave fig leaves together, hide behind them, and call it art. God loves all true and beautiful art (including the loveliness of a fig leaf), but He does not delight in beauty that is not matched to a life of love.

Apparently Lucifer was the most beautiful of angels … but God did not delight in his beauty.

The question is this: Do our lives reflect the beauty, love, and justice of God? That's a tough question to answer honestly. I wish the question was this instead: Does our music reflect the beauty, love, and justice of God? Answering that affirmatively can be done a whole lot easier than saying that our lives match the words of our songs.

Because God knows and sees everything, there is a day of reckoning coming. In the Scriptures it's called "the day of the Lord." Whether that day is a day of terror or a day of delight for us depends on how we live our lives.

In the book of Revelation there is an account of what people who have not repented of their sins and received the love of God will cry out. This will be the cry of those who have spent their earthly lives selfishly delighting only themselves:

> Then the kings of the earth, the princes, the generals, the rich, the mighty, and every slave and every free man hid in caves and among the rocks of the mountains. They called to the mountains and the rocks, "Fall on us and hide us from the face of him who sits on the throne and from the wrath of the Lamb! For the great day of their wrath has come, and who can stand?" (Rev. 6:15–17)

It's interesting to me that it doesn't say "the wrath of the Lion of the tribe of Judah." No, it says the "wrath of the Lamb"! If the image of wrath was connected to a lion, it wouldn't be too surprising—we have seen or heard of the wrath of lions as they rip apart their prey.

But the wrath of a lamb?

Maybe the kings of the earth were expecting a lion but were surprised by a lamb. When the Lamb of God came the first time, the Jews were surprised too, because He didn't conquer the Romans. The Jews expected a lion of a Messiah, but He came as a lamb.

It says of this lamb that a "smoldering wick he will not snuff out" and a "bruised reed he will not break" (Isa. 42:3). The Lamb of God is the love of God. He is the compassion of God incarnate.

But love is not love if there is no justice and payment for sin. It will fall to the Lamb to pass judgment, and that is good news for all of us. All of God's wrath will pass through Jesus, the Lamb of God, who identifies with our human struggles yet was without sin.

So why couldn't the kings of the earth stand before the Lamb?

They knew that they had lived lives of wickedness and that the day of accounting had come. All of a sudden, what they had never wanted to admit to themselves or anyone else before became totally clear.

God knows everything about me.

He knows every thought and deed. He knows every time I have sinned against someone else.

He knows.

And that is the incredible thing about God's judgment and justice. It will be complete and total. It will be perfect. No amazing lawyer will be able to use convincing arguments to get anyone out of jail. The time for hiding and pretending will be over. Every unsolved crime will be brought to light and justice. Every horrific deed will be accounted for, and justice will be delivered.

Because God knows everything.

And that is also the incredible thing about God's love and mercy—it is complete and total. It is perfect; it casts out all fear. The time for hiding and pretending is over. And on that day no crafty demon or person will be able to separate us from the love of God.

Every insecurity and doubt will be swallowed up in the light and love of God.

And even now, in the time before the incredible day of the Lord, we can experience unconditional love.

The love that makes us sing.

There is a powerful hymn that is not universally known but that is one of my favorites. I learned it as a child when my dad led the singing in our Mennonite church.

The Love of God

The love of God is greater far than tongue or pen could ever tell;
It goes beyond the highest star, and reaches to the lowest hell;
The guilty pair, bowed down with care, God gave His Son to win;
His erring child, He reconciled, and pardoned from his sin.

O love of God, how rich and pure! How measureless and strong!
It shall forevermore endure, the saints' and angels' song.

Could we with ink the ocean fill,
and were the skies of parchment made,
Were every stalk on earth a quill, and every man a scribe by trade,
To write the love of God above, would drain the ocean dry.
Nor could the scroll contain the whole,
though stretched from sky to sky.

O love of God, how rich and pure! How measureless and strong!
It shall forevermore endure, the saints' and angels' song.[3]

I love the fact that F. M. Lehman says that tongue or pen can never tell the depths of God's love ... but then he does what all creative people do and has a go at it! And the songwriter does an amazing job, using the images of an ocean filled with ink, the skies made of parchment, every stalk on earth a old-fashioned writing utensil waiting to be filled with ink—and every man setting out to write. The writers drain the ocean and fill the sky, and the job is still not done!

It's an impossibly big picture. And it should be, because God's love is impossibly bigger than we could ever imagine.

Maybe when I grow up, I will write some lyrics that come within a country mile of that kind of grandeur! In the meantime we song-writers have to continue trying to write God songs filled with God words. Some people complain that there are too many new songs being written. They said the same thing with the whole hymn explosion a couple of hundred years ago. The same thing will happen yet again, and the best songs will endure!

We need to keep writing and singing songs about who God is and what He is doing. That's not just something we will be doing while we are earthbound. I wonder what kind of new love songs we will be singing in eternity. The images will be amazing ... and the songs even more so.

I wonder what God words we will be singing then.

SONGWRITING TIPS

Be prepared to write songs anytime, anywhere—even if you are looking after your squalling child. Okay, that's a little unusual, but it happened to me! I think sometimes we believe that to write good songs and be effective in our creativity, we have to separate ourselves completely from the world and noise and distractions. Sometimes that's a good and right thing to do. But sometimes it's not necessary. I was recently working on a song with Kathryn Scott; she started writing it in a busy airport and recorded the melodic idea amid the din of airport noise.

My wife sometimes blesses me to go away for a couple of days to retreat and write. But occasionally, if I ask her for the opportunity, she looks at me with a twinkle in her eye and just says, "Hallelujah!" I know what she is saying—that even in the middle of crazy family life God can give good creative gifts!

Sing God words. There are a number of God words found in the Scriptures. Study their root meanings, dive into the depth of what they mean, and then find a way to sing them.

Don't dismiss an idea because it sounds too simple. That's what Brenton initially did when I sang out the idea (and I don't blame him considering the circumstances!). Of course, the key thing is figuring out whether the idea is simple and bad or simple and great!

If you can't finish a song, embrace the joy and challenges of cowriting. Sometimes you keep coming back to a song—you really believe that one section is strong, but you can't seem to finish it. Listen for God's direction to partner with someone else. And by the way, that cowriting partner is not your favorite songwriter whom you don't know and don't have access to; it's someone in your circle of relationships.

Be prepared to live the songs that you are writing. To me this is one of the biggest downers of mainstream music. Most of the time the singers and songwriters are acting (sadly some of them are not; they are living out their sensual and immoral songs!). They will say things like, "It's only a song."

God intends us to live our songs. So I want to challenge each songwriter to write songs—but more importantly I want to challenge all writers to live their songs … and if you can't live your songs, maybe you need to change your life, and maybe you need to change your songs!

Notes

1. Brenton Brown and Brian Doerksen, "Hallelujah (Your Love Is Amazing)," © 2000 Vineyard Songs (UK/Eire). Used by permission.

2. Most of this information on the root meanings of *hallelujah* comes from Dorothy Peters, a Hebrew scholar and Dead Sea Scrolls specialist—who also happens to be my wife's sister!

3. F. M. Lehman, "The Love of God."

It's Time for the Reign of God

It's time for the reign of God
It's time for Your light to shine
It's time for the kingdom of our God to be revealed

It's time for authority
It's time for Your majesty
It's time for the kingdom of our God to be revealed

In these days of wars and famines
In these days when hearts grow cold
In these days of growing darkness
There's a story to be told

So we gather in the Spirit
Lift up a prayer of faith
We proclaim the mighty Word of God
The power in Your name

For the captives of rebellion
Addicted and deceived
For those who wander far from home
It's time to intercede

So we gather in the Spirit
Lift up a prayer of faith
We proclaim the mighty Word of God
The power in Your name; the power in Your name![1]

CHAPTER 10

It's Time for the Reign of God

When you hear the word *time,* what comes to your mind? Seconds … minutes … hours …days? Or something seasonal, something less about precise measurements? There are two main words for time from the New Testament era. *Chronos* is all about linear time; one measurable moment follows another until our days and lives are full. Then there's the word *kairos*—that time when God's purposes are fulfilled.

Time is both *chronos* and *kairos,* but perhaps its ebb and flow shouldn't be measured out mainly in seconds but in seasons. Maybe that's how God wants us as humans to live—more engaged in each season and less anxious about maximizing each minute.

In Paul's letter to the Galatian church he writes, "But when the fullness of the time came, God sent forth His Son" (Gal. 4:4 nasb).

I love the words *fullness* and *time* brought side by side.

God … waiting until everything was ready and in place.

God … waiting until history got filled up and releasing His kingdom at just the right time.

Paul was saying that it was the right time for Jesus to enter the world. I don't think he was talking about a specific minute and possibly not even the exact day of His birth. (For sure he wasn't talking about all the technical measurements that come along with a birth in our modern age.) We don't know the exact day or hour when Jesus was born; we know the approximate year (give or take a few!). But I think Paul was talking about a season in history.

When Paul spoke in Athens on one of his missionary journeys, he gave these powerful and true words: "From one man he made every nation of men, that they should inhabit the whole earth; and he determined the times set for them and the exact places where they should live. God did this so that men would seek him and perhaps reach out for him and find him, though he is not far from each one of us. 'For in him we live and move and have our being'" (Acts 17:26–28).

The times are set for us. Our calling is to step into what God has planned for us.[2]

When Paul used the words *fullness* and *time,* one of the things he wanted us to think about was a healthy pregnancy. A woman filled with life, loved and prepared to bring that life into this world, is so radiant and beautiful. My wife went through that five times in order to birth our six children; what a beautiful mother she was ... and still is!

Recently I have felt a stirring in my spirit. Could it be that we are entering another season where the church is almost pregnant with the purposes of God—a new season where the life of the kingdom of God will break into our world again? It's not time for another Messiah—He already came, lived, died, and rose from the dead! I'm talking about another release of the rule and reign of God—a season where the things Jesus came to release in the first century come into focus and are released again with authority and love.

We are not in charge of exactly when that's going to happen, just as a woman can't determine the precise minute she will give birth naturally—she just knows the season. We're also not in charge of exactly what the next release of the kingdom is going to look like, just as a mother doesn't know the details of her baby's appearance. We are not in charge of many things ... but it's so good for us to lean into the hope of the coming kingdom and fill our hearts with expectancy of what God longs to do. There were many people in the first century who missed the reign of God among them because it looked different from their expectations. Expectation is such a wonderful thing—but we must always mix our expectation with surrender to the things that are out of our control. And expectation must ultimately be put on the One who created everything and knows the path to life.

This song is about the season we are in as believers around the world—a season where we are expecting the reign of God to be poured out on the earth again. And often that expectation and longing comes in the middle of seasons of great difficulty.

About six months before I wrote this song, we went through the painful process of being involved in a church split. I never thought I would be involved in something so confusing and excruciating in the middle of the church, the place intended by God to be a family and an army, the place where we are healed from the wounds we receive on the battlefield of life. The split was presented as positively as possible in our community, but the reality of what happened—if you were on the inside—was very painful and confusing for everyone. Why did it happen? I've struggled with laying a big chunk of the blame at my feet, for I know that as a human, I made some mistakes along the way. I was the leader of the pastoral search group, so I was the one who introduced our new pastors to our church. I thought they were doing a wonderful job, but after a little over a year of ministry, several leaders on the church board expressed their disappointment with this pastoral couple; they didn't like their "style" and didn't feel they had the spiritual authority to be our pastors. They also did not agree with my leadership decisions, especially my love and support of our new pastors. After several months of agonizing and difficult meetings, which included my resignation from the church board, of which I was the leader for over a year, the remaining board members fired the pastors. We were devastated! Why didn't we see this coming when I first introduced this new couple to the church's existing leadership? And why wouldn't this group of people let go of what was and press into the future with this new couple?

But out of the pain, something was born. We regrouped with several old and new friends, including this new pastoral couple that we loved so much. The truth is, we respected them even more after we saw how they handled the crisis with such grace and character. As a team we planted a new nondenominational church called The Bridge.[3] The church started with fairly traumatic labor … but a few years later the pain of that birth is far behind us, and we are having the time of our lives doing local ministry with great friends.

It was in this season—about six months after the start of our new church—that my good friend Steve Mitchinson and I went to Mayne Island for a few days of retreat. When you drive off the ferry onto the island, it's as if time slows down. Those Southern Gulf Islands have a whole different pace of life, making them a wonderful place to go rest and be creative without distractions. We were staying at my sister-in-law's cabin and writing songs, and after a couple of days of writing and sharing hearts, we were almost out of time. Steve said, "We have time for one more ... what do you want to write about?" To be honest, I felt done. I didn't have the energy to write anymore. I didn't want to be creative at that moment. But when your friend has faith and energy for one more ... you go for it and do one more!

I pulled out a file of songwriting ideas, and my eyes fell on a phrase that I had written down several years ago. All that was on the paper was one phrase—*It's time for the reign of God.*

As soon as I spoke the words out loud, I knew—we needed to sing it! So I opened my mouth in faith and started to find the melody and rhythm that matched the phrase ... and within moments I had the core idea, and we were off. It's amazing how revelation and creativity can wake me up from my lethargy! And when I start singing about the kingdom of God, I get excited. I get focused.

The kingdom of God was always on the lips of Jesus, because the kingdom of God is what ruled in His heart.[4]

God exercises His rule and reign in the kingdom—and it starts in the heart. All other kingdoms start with physical borders and external laws; God's kingdom alone changes the human heart. And since God is the creator of our hearts, of all our inner lives and emotions, He alone can penetrate and change us from the inside out.[5]

But religion never gets the "inside out" thing. Just the other day I heard an interview with freedom fighters in Pakistan. They are willing to lay down their arms and cease from armed struggle *if* the nation accepts Sharia—a code of law based on the Qur'an and teachings of Muhammad. For example, women need to be covered head to foot with a burka in public, and men should show their devotion to Islam with a full beard. As I listened, I realized again that every religious structure and reign outside of what Jesus released is a counterfeit of the kingdom of God. Sharia is built upon external obedience (for example, women must be covered). This type of kingdom reign will never succeed in releasing life and provision to people. It exchanges one type of bondage for another. And sadly it's not just happening in countries under the crescent moon of Islam. It's happened throughout the history of Christian nations and is happening right now in Israel.

I just read on CNN.com about a fourteen-year-old-girl from the Jewish town of Beitar Illit who was attacked and had acid thrown onto her face, legs, and stomach. Why was she attacked? Because she was wearing loose-fitting pants and a short-sleeved shirt—attire considered immodest by the town's ultraorthodox modesty guard.

This kind of thing has gone on in religion since the beginning of time—a mixture of religious zeal and a focus on appearances—and it's a deadly combination. Religious leaders trying to police people … by enforcing external rules. What a bad combination!

Jesus came to release the reign of God, which was always meant to be a reign of life and love, not a reign of terror and fear! Jesus didn't run around like a bully trying to get people to "behave or else." (Think about the story of the woman caught in adultery!) Jesus invited all who would listen to be changed from the inside out.

The kingdom of God may start in the heart, but it will lead to a release of authority—God's decisive will and power to act on behalf of people. So much of the spirit of this age involves a move away from authority. This shift comes partly because we hear about things like Sharia law, and we don't want that type of authority. Nor are we as Christians proud of much of our history, where church leaders abused their authority and used their position to take instead of give. We need authority, and we need it desperately—but we need the right authority. God's authority. His authority is always given in grace and exercised in love. It's time for authority!

It's also time for majesty—the revelation and release of God's beauty. The kingdom of God is not just about order; it's also about creative beauty. In our rush for function over form in the last century (just look at most of the buildings that were designed and built after World War II, and you'll see what I mean), we have discarded and disregarded our need for beauty. The kingdom of God is not like that. We need beauty in our lives to truly live. And there is none more beautiful than God Himself.

I love David's description in Psalm 27 as he seeks the beauty of God above all else.

> One thing I ask of the Lord, this is what I seek: that I may dwell
> in the house of the Lord all the days of my life, to gaze upon the
> beauty of the Lord and to seek him in his temple. (v. 4)

David was a seeker of God's beauty, submitted to God's authority. He was a worshipper … and I want to be more like Dave!

At the heart of the reign of God is a kingdom of worshippers—and what other response should there be to God drawing near in His kingdom but worship? And so we gather in the Spirit to worship … to pray … to proclaim the Word of God. The Enemy wants to scatter us, to cut us off from each other and from God. When we gather, we place ourselves under the authority of God's Word and the inspiration of the Holy Spirit. We come together so that we can be empowered to go.

And as we go, we bring healing and justice to those who are oppressed; we bring freedom to the prisoners.

One of the most encouraging moments in my ministry happened recently on a trip into the local prison to lead worship and meet with some of the inmates. We had poured out our hearts in worship and declared the Word of God. We had finished the gathering and were about to leave when one of the inmates stood up in the back and said something like, "Before you leave, there is something we want to say to you—for the past ninety minutes … you have given us the gift of freedom. Thank you!"

The gift of freedom … isn't that what the reign of God releases?

Who needs the reign of God? Who needs freedom?

Everyone!

We all need it … but those who are captive to other kingdoms need it the most! And issues like child abuse, pornography, drug addiction, and extreme poverty and hunger are symptoms of people living under the rule and reign of kingdoms apart from God.

Just this morning, as I was eating breakfast, I was thinking how grateful I am to have food to eat … and then I thought, *Wouldn't it be great if each of us with food could share that food with the hungry?* In my mind I pictured people coming to our home. In my mind I saw a Chinese couple and their one child, a few African children who have lost their parents to AIDS, some Asian refugees, and several Mexican workers—people from different nations coming to my door. What a joy it would be to feed them, to hear their stories, and to help them on their journeys. If only it were that simple ... but they can't get to my door. People from the other side of the world can't drop in and share my bowl of granola; they need to be fed where they live.[6] And why aren't they being fed enough where they live?

Many times they are not being fed because they are under the authority of corrupt governments—people who are not using their power to serve, but rather to be served. The reign they are under is not the reign of God!

Think about North Korea: a handful of leaders living in luxury while much of the country is at the point of starvation.

Journalists who followed Kim Jong-Il on a recent trip through Russia reported some of the excesses: He was drinking bottles of Bordeaux, burgundy, and cognac worth $650 a bottle and consuming dinners that ran up to twenty courses. In North Korea he uses slave labor to mine for gold and then stashes away billions in Swiss accounts while his people starve. The country under his reign experiences constant food shortages. I long to feed those people ... but I can't. If we send food aid, most of it ends up in the wrong hands and never reaches those who are truly hungry!

We could list a number of other tyrants around the world living lives of incredible luxury while oppressing their own people.

Who our authority is determines whether we get fed!

Being fed is connected to spiritual authority. If there is good spiritual authority, then God releases His blessing and provision. If the authority is self-serving, we go hungry.

In the Old Testament, God made it clear that if His people followed Him and His ways, there would be food to spare—food to share. But if they allowed their devotion to wander to other gods, even their land would pay the price; their crops would fail, and they would go hungry.

We were created not only to have enough for ourselves, but also to share our provision with others—for as we do that, we are living out the character of the One in whose image we are made.

God is a giver, and we come to life and become more like Him when we give!

Can you get a sense of what is at stake?

When we sing, "It's time for the reign of God," we are declaring that life or death is at stake. If we come under the reign of God, we live; if we come under the reign of humanity and all of the wickedness of the kingdoms of this world, we die.

Thanks be to God, who is still reaching out to bring us under His rule and reign! It's under the reign of the kingdom of God that we live life to the fullest. And isn't that what we are all longing for—to really live? We as humans yearn for life … and that yearning is meant to find its fulfillment in the kingdom of God. Why do we yearn for the reign of God? There are so many reasons.

We Were Created for Justice

When we experience or see injustice, we are horrified … and we should be! It's a sign of the kingdom of God to speak out against injustice and to act justly: "He has showed you, O man, what is good. And what does the Lord require of you? To act justly and to love mercy and to walk humbly with your God" (Mic. 6:8).

We Were Created for Light

There is a powerful description in Revelation about our future destination—we are going to dwell in a place filled with light, a place with no more night: "There will be no more night. They will not need the light of a lamp or the light of the sun, for the Lord God will give them light. And they will reign for ever and ever" (Rev. 22:5).

This reference to night strikes me afresh right now—mainly because in the last few weeks I haven't been feeling 100 percent, and I'm not getting enough sleep. The need to sleep and rest will be over because we will be with the One who is eternal strength. I am overcome with emotion and tears even as I write these words—what kind of kingdom are we being invited into? A kingdom that has such love and power that we won't need to sleep anymore … that's incredible! An amazing adventure awaits!

The night also stirs up images of the kingdoms of man—the domains of darkness where evil rules from the shadows. No more reigns of darkness … just light! And did you notice that the verse states that "they will reign." It's not just God who will reign—He brings His servants into His reign. Our future destiny is to join God in His reign.[7] This is just over the top—what amazing adventures are waiting for us!

We Were Created to Walk with God[8]

When man and woman walked with God in the garden of Eden, they were fully under the reign of God. They trusted God and were surrendered to His authority. This is what we were created for—and so this is what we yearn to experience again. And while we cannot return to that garden (avoiding the cross by returning to the garden of Eden is one of the favorite lies of so many of the New Age teachers), we were created to walk with God, to hear His voice. Jesus came to restore to us this intimate friendship and relationship with our Creator.

And here is another area where the reign of God is totally different from the reign of people. How many earthly kings can you have relationship with? Probably none. And if you could, would you even want to know them for anything beyond what they could do for you? Most of them grasp for power and are not people full of grace. The only people they welcome are people who make them look good!

Yet the King who reigns over us longs for us to be close to Him. He gives us full access to relationship with Him. We are His sons and daughters, and so we are welcomed right into His throne room.

Do you remember the picture of John F. Kennedy in the Oval Office with his son, John, sitting under the Resolute desk? While his father was doing the work of the president, John was playing under the desk. He had that kind of access because he was his son.

That's the kind of access we have to our Father's presence.

When was the last time you played so casually in the Father's house? This is one of the many things I love about my special-needs son Isaiah: He just loves to play and often is totally relaxed playing with his trains by my feet while I … well, I am concerned about so many things.

Okay. I know it's hard sometimes to fully experience the access we have to our Father because we can't go into His presence physically while we remain earthbound. When we cross over through the curtain of death, we will be fully there. Yet I have experienced being in the Father's presence now in faith, and I believe that He is more than willing to make His presence known to us as we surrender to His rule and reign. That's why worship feels like coming home—we enter the presence of God, and we are at home with our Father. It's in worship that our hearts are as satisfied as they ever will be in this life … so can you imagine what worship will be like on the other side? When He wipes away every tear from our eyes?

Some days I feel like I am going to combust with the fiery desire in me for that reality.

The Reign of Man Will Never Satisfy Our Thirst for All of the Above

No matter how good an earthly king, president, prime minister, or any other authority figure is, he or she can never fully satisfy our longings for justice, protection, and provision. No matter how amazing a country is (and I happen to be very grateful to be a Canadian!), it's not nearly amazing enough to fill up our hearts completely. God put "eternity in [our] hearts" (Eccl. 3:11)—how could a country of any earthly ruler ever fill that up? I remember distinctly a moment when we were living in London, England, about ten years ago. London has always been one of my favorite places on the planet for many reasons, but as I walked through London that day and looked at all the beautiful buildings (although, along with the beauty, I smelled the pollution and heard the screeching black cabs), I declared out loud, "Thank You, Lord, for bringing me and my family to London for this season … I'm so grateful … but, Lord … I long for Your city—how long until I can dwell there?"

God's Reign Releases Provision That Comes without a Sting

It's amazing to me how the provision of God always is accompanied by peace. Humanity's supply often comes with a sting … and strings attached that bind people. (Maybe we should print a bumper sticker that goes something like this: Trust God for your provision—there's no sting or strings attached!)

One of the great tragedies of North American history is how white people from Europe treated the native peoples. One of the things they forced the natives to do was send their children to residential schools— separating them from their families and customs to give them a "real" education. While they were there, many of the native children were given an education not only in science and math, but also in physical and sexual abuse. In some recent victories for the victims, the abused were given large financial settlements to compensate for their suffering. Justice was served! The only problem is humanity's idea of justice often involves simply writing someone a check—and that provision comes with a sting. Now many of these abuse victims are dying, not from the hands of their abusers, but from their own hands. They are spending the money they received as compensation on alcohol and drugs and are killing themselves with substance abuse.

Many of the First Nations peoples have rejected Christianity because of its association with the abusers and their residential schools. Some of the abusers may have been Christian in name, but they were far from Christ in heart and action.

How the First Nations peoples of North America need the reign of God now, just like they needed it five hundred years ago! For even prior to the arrival of the Europeans, many of those nations were at war with one another as they fought for the right to reign. Many of them experienced great suffering at the hand of another nation prior to suffering under the reign of the European settlers.[9]

When God pours out His reign, He longs to do it in a way that honors our unique cultures. He wants to make His ways known among us. He gives us freedom to create our various cultures as human beings, and then He steps into the middle of that culture and reveals Himself. He wants to awaken our hearts so we can be fully alive, fully and uniquely who He has created us to be!

And one of the most powerful ways to awaken hearts is through redemptive stories. That's why I used this line in the song: "There's a story to be told."

It's time for the epic stories of God to be told in every possible way—to the children while their hearts are young and their minds are like a sponge; to the teenagers who are longing for adventure and considering wandering away from the faith of their mothers and fathers; to every generation. All people need to hear the grand God stories … and hear them again.

And that means we need to use every communication medium we've got! All of the arts and all technology.

The world is being bombarded with information. Why don't we fill the world with stories? God stories … creative redemptive stories that inspire us to live life God's way.

As I write this, we are just finishing up an over seven-year journey of writing a musical version of one of the most-loved stories of all time: the Luke 15 story of a father and his two sons. We are telling the story of the Prodigal Son's journey through the eyes of the elder brother—and of course through the eyes of their brokenhearted, wastefully extravagant father. Stories like this make my heart ache for the kingdom of God to be revealed in our time.

And so the next time you sing, "It's time for the reign of God," let your heart resonate with all of these truths. These are the things we are declaring; these are the things we are surrendering to when we come under the reign of God. And if you are tired … out of strength … out of energy … maybe even out of time, then remember—that's just how I felt on the day I started writing this song. Just maybe your best days are still ahead of you. For when the reign of God falls on our lives, we are renewed, and even older guys like me mount up on wings like eagles and soar!

SONGWRITING TIPS

Keep a file of song ideas that you can revisit when you draw away to write songs. If all you have is a lyrical phrase, don't forget it. Write it down. It may come back around years later when you know what to do with it. That's why this song exists. One day I had the idea to write a song called "It's Time for the Reign of God," but that's all I had—an idea. Several years later we wrote the song.

Start the songwriting process by speaking the words out loud. This is how you tell whether these words are on fire and can be shaped into a song. You start with speaking ... then you move to chanting—finding a simple melody for that phrase and repeating it until you believe it!

Embrace the unique DNA of each song idea. One of the interesting things about the whole writing process is that each song is unique. You can't copy a previous song because there is something unique at the core of the new song that is setting a fresh direction. This song just sort of came out as a "country rock" song (which isn't my thing—I grew up loving bands like U2!). The core idea of the song helps determine what the song becomes—kind of like DNA.

Make sure people can remember and know what the song is called. You do this through key phrase placement and repetition. Your title is like the handle: It's what people who are looking for a song reach out for and take hold of.

Surprise people with some fresh words ... and then give them enough familiar words around the fresh words that you don't lose your congregation. In this song I start verse two with a section about those who really need the reign of God ... and I'm guessing that you haven't sung about "the captives of rebellion, addicted and deceived" that often in your church. But I return to the simple "so we gather in the Spirit."

Notes

1. "It's Time for the Reign of God" by Brian Doerksen & Steve Mitchinson © 2007 Integrity's Hosanna! Music/ASCAP & Shining Rose Songs (adm by Integrity's Hosanna! Music)/ASCAP & Ion Publishing (adm by Vineyard Music). Used by permission.

2. One could argue from Psalm 139:16 that even the day of our birth is planned: "All the days ordained for me were written in your book before one of them came to be."

3. See www.thebridgeonline.ca.

4. "For out of the overflow of his heart his mouth speaks." (Luke 6:45)

5. I have a song on that theme called "Change Me on the Inside," which is recorded on my *Holy God* CD.

6. I do believe in relief care for nations struck by poverty and calamity, and I participate in those efforts.

7. That does not mean that we will become "God"—no, we are still finite, for we had a beginning. God remains in His triune Being the only One completely outside of time: "From everlasting to everlasting you are God" (see Ps. 90:1–2). Hey, that sounds like a good idea for a song!

8. John Eldredge has a wonderful book on this subject aptly called *Walking with God.*

9. Of course there are many wonderful exceptions to negative reigns among the First Nations and the Europeans who came. In every situation there always seems to be a light shining, keeping our yearning for the kingdom of God alive!

With All My Affection

With all my affection
All my understanding
Lord, I worship You

With my every action
All my spirit's passion
Lord, I worship You

There's no higher call
Than loving You with my life
There's no higher ground
Than kneeling down before You
Lord I surrender
I worship[1]

CHAPTER 11

With All My Affection

People have filled the air with worship songs for thousands of years. And whatever word the language or culture used to express the concept of worship, people continuously lifted up that word into the heavens in song or prayer. But when we say or sing the words "I worship," do we really know and comprehend what we are saying? Should we even say it at all, or is it simply something to live?

As a worship leader and songwriter, I actually have an aversion to worship songs using the word "worship" in them. (As soon as I say that, I must immediately confess that on a couple of songs like this one, I have used the word, because it felt like the only word I could use.) My aversion comes from wanting to avoid the "I've said it so I've done it" mentality that can creep into modern worship services.

To "do worship," we need to willingly surrender all we are to all God is.

It's impossible for that to be contained in a song or in a worship service that lasts an hour or two. To surrender all we are takes our entire lives, and getting to know God fully is going to take eternity.

Some people get scared when they hear they'll be worshipping forever. Maybe they don't like singing, and they were told that eternity is one continuous sing-along! I believe eternity will be one continuous adventure … and I believe that songs and acts of worship will be woven into the adventure. I don't really know what it's going to look like, but it's going to be better than anything we could imagine or dream up!

> No eye has seen, no ear has heard,
> and no mind has imagined
> what God has prepared for those who love him.
> (1 Cor. 2:9 NLT)

God is preparing some amazing things that we can't even imagine—sounds like more than just singing some songs, doesn't it? (Though I hope the sheer ecstasy of being immersed in some magnificent music is part of it!)[2]

Who is He preparing these things for? Those who *love* Him! That's a pretty compelling reason to keep "loving God" at the top of our lists and in the center of our hearts.

The heart of worship is loving God. And just like the word *love* means more than just sentimental feelings, so the word *worship* is a grand, robust word meaning so much more than singing. True worship springs from our affections and is confirmed by our actions.

It is anchored by our understanding and sustained by our spiritual passion.

Worship is living out the words of Jesus quoted from the Torah: "Love the Lord your God with all your heart and with all your soul and with all your mind and with all your strength" (Mark 12:30).[3]

So if worship is much more than singing a song, what is it specifically, and how can we grow in it? Answering those questions is a big challenge! Worship is almost impossible to define or contain. Maybe instead of defining worship, we should describe it. To define something, one narrows it down using as few words as possible. To describe something, one uses many words to depict it. Within the word *describe* is a "scribe"—someone who is compelled to write.

Let me try to describe worship, knowing that I am only scribing it in part.

Worship is surrender, deeply and completely from the heart.

Worship is abandon … letting go of our self to focus on God.

Worship is laying down our resistance, inviting God's reign to invade our lives.

Our surrender doesn't come from being overpowered, but rather from being overwhelmed; it's a surrender to the love of God. Think about that for a moment. God didn't send a massive army to conquer us. He sent His Son to be born in an animal feeding trough. Jesus lived a life of love and gave up all His rights so that we might see what God is like. God sent love willingly so that we might respond with love willingly. We relinquish our rights not because we have to, but because we want to! What makes worship work is our "want to," not our "have to." If it's not willing worship, it's not worship.

Worship is brokenness—a breaking of our will: *Thy will be done.* The first use of the word *worship* happens on Mount Moriah. The cruelty and kindness of God wrapped up in this story are staggering! To modern observers, the demand to sacrifice Isaac seems unusually cruel. Yet in that time and culture, human sacrifice was part of the ancient religions.[4] I am sure that Abraham knew in his spirit that YHWH was different from the other gods, but as he trekked for three days to the mountain that God would show him, how could he know for sure? To find out meant completely abandoning himself to this God who was speaking to him and trusting Him totally, withholding nothing.

The test that God initiates with Abraham is designed to break him of all self-will and self-effort, to rid him of any human striving to fulfill the covenant promises of God. Placing his son upon the altar clearly meant, "Lay down your future!" This would show God that Abraham's trust and willingness to obey were absolute and total.

Total submission to the test.

What could initially be seen as cruelty we see now as a clear, prophetic foreshadowing of another sacrificial act of worship that happened on Mount Moriah centuries later.[5] But Abraham did not have our vantage point. He couldn't see the outcome and the way that his act of total obedience would so clearly point to the Lamb of God, who takes away the sin of the world.

Just before father and son arrived at the altar, Isaac asked, "Where is the lamb for the burnt offering?" (Gen. 22:7). From the beginning God revealed to His people that an unblemished lamb was needed to atone for sin.

And at the very moment of Abraham's absolute obedience, God released His provision: "Abraham looked up and there in a thicket he saw a ram" (Gen. 22:13).

Just as God provided a ram on Mount Moriah, He provided a sacrifice to save us from our sins.

> John saw Jesus coming toward him and said, "Look, the Lamb
> of God, who takes away the sin of the world!" (John 1:29)

Recently I cowrote a song with Kathryn Scott. It's called "Thank You for the Cross," and in the prechorus we lift up this cry based on these two moments in Scripture: "Look the Lamb of God who takes away our sin."[6]

On the top of Mount Moriah, the angel says something so wonderful to Abraham: "You have not withheld from me even your son, your only son" (Gen. 22:12 nlt).

What a powerful description of what it means to worship God! Worship is our expression of releasing everything to God, withholding nothing from the altar of God.

All other gods and religions ask only for parts or pieces, often expressed in rituals and rites. Once we have given part, we can do whatever we want with the rest of our lives. But YHWH has the audacity to ask for it all.

Could God say to each of us, "You have withheld nothing from Me"? That's what it means to be a worshipper of God!

Abraham was the first one to show us that worship is *physical.* It involves all we are. It's an act of obedience, a living sacrifice; we place our bodies on the altar of God. Worship is staying on the altar even though everything within us wants to get up and resume control of our own lives. Worship is realizing that we are no longer our own; we belong to Him!

> Therefore, I urge you, brothers, in view of God's mercy, to offer your bodies as living sacrifices, holy and pleasing to God—this is your spiritual act of worship. (Rom. 12:1)

Worship is spiritual. It's a response to a spiritual call that is initiated by God: "Deep calls to deep" (Ps. 42:7). Have you ever tried to explain worship to someone who has no interest in spiritual things? Someone who believes that life is only physical and that we are the result of an explosion and subsequent evolution? I have had a couple of interesting conversations with customs officials when I cross international borders. When they ask what I do, I tell them, "I'm a worship leader and songwriter." They can grasp the songwriter bit, but a worship leader? If I was crossing a border in ancient times and told them that I was a worship leader, the response may have been, "Which god?" In the Western world we seem to have lost the insight that all of us are worshippers. Worship makes no sense to those who are not awakened spiritually.

Worship is emotional. It awakens the core of our emotions and turns them "godward." Worship is not mere intellectual assent of truth. It involves our hearts coming in agreement with God, and that agreement causes our feelings to follow. If we never get emotional in following and loving God, are we really worshipping?

Worship is the expression of our deepest affections—and there is nothing that shapes our lives more than our affections. In fact the things and people we have affection for rule our lives. Our affections are like the wheel that turns the rudder of a ship. They set the course of our lives. There is nothing or no one more worthy of affection than God. And our hearts and affections need to be protected. Listen to this warning: "Above all else, guard your heart, for it is the wellspring of life" (Prov. 4:23).

Even the very first of the Ten Commandments—"You shall have no other gods before Me" (Ex. 20:3 nasb)—makes sense when you think about this from God's perspective. God knows He is the only one worthy of our devotion and love, and so He invites us to be ruled by Him alone, because He is the only ruler who is truly good! We will be ruled by someone or something. As Bob Dylan sang so well (actually his voice is terrible, but his words are powerfully true!): "You gotta serve somebody."

Worship is found in that moment when we realize that God is God and we are not—and we're okay with that. The problem of human history is that when we find out that we are not God, we are not okay with that. And that's why Satan fell eons ago—he was not okay with not being God!

Worship is dangerous. It reveals our rebellion. When we worship, our self-will is revealed, and we are called to repent of our rebellion against God. That process of repentance goes by another name: *change*. And we don't like change. So to lead or engage in biblical worship is always a dangerous endeavor.

Worship is drawing near to the God who is a consuming fire. It's living in the fear of the Lord. That means a radical respect and reverence for God. It's not flippant! Living in the fear of the Lord means much more than removing your hat when you pray, like some men do. It's true that certain traditions of respect are eroding in our culture. It's sad to see them go. But to have a few rituals of respect scattered throughout our social lives—and to then believe that those things make us good Christians—misses the mark by a mile. People who don't pray often talk differently when they do. They try to elevate their language to make it sound more reverent. That's not what I mean by living in the fear of the Lord! The fear of the Lord is a reverence for God that saturates every aspect of our lives, yet is lived out in a natural and relational way. You don't have to become a hermit or join a monastery or convent to live in the fear of the Lord.

Worship is relationship. It's entering the Trinity's eternal communion. And within the nature of the triune God, Jesus goes before us and intercedes for us. Jesus is our worship leader.

Worship is resting from our own works and entering into His. Worship begins not with frantic doing, but in peaceful receiving. For this reason I will often start a gathering of worship with something gentle about our receiving from God instead of a big praise anthem. The psalmist expressed it this way: "Cease striving and know that I am God" (Ps. 46:10 nasb).

Worship remembers God's epic story of salvation. Worship tells the salvation story in fresh and ancient ways so we never forget the story! *Zakar,* the Hebrew command to remember, is one of the most important and needed commands in Scripture—it is found over one hundred times in the Old Testament alone.

Worship is a celebration of gratitude. It's our outpouring of thanksgiving, and that thanksgiving releases our celebration. Worship is gratitude for who God is and all He has done—and it's meant to be a party! So much of the world's fun is about gratifying our physical senses in a way that is completely self-serving. I'm reminded of casinos in places like Las Vegas—they promise "Fun! Fun! Fun!" but the promises are empty. I can't think of anything more thrilling than the release of celebration that occurs when we worship God with all our hearts, like David did, knowing that our lives are blessing God and those around us!

Finally, as I am sure you can tell from all I am describing, *worship has nothing to do with music.* You don't need music to worship. But you do need understanding.

Our understanding of who God is and how the world works affects everything about our lives. We are called to love God with our hearts and with our minds. We worship through our clear biblical understanding of who God is.

In other words, our thinking matters.

The content and theology in each worship song is vital! And not just the theological content of each individual song—the theological emphasis of our overall song list, the songs and hymns that we sing the most, is incredibly important. That emphasis reveals what we really believe about who God is.

I will never forget the day that Dr. Gordon Fee came to our church and said, "Show me your songbook, and I will write your theology." It struck me in that moment—we send people away to Bible school and seminary for years to learn the Scriptures and how to preach. And upon their return they preach sermons, which people often promptly forget. But there are very few theological schools designed to help modern artists and worship songwriters learn the Scriptures and biblical theology; we just tell them to write us a song we can sing in church. Maybe it's the songwriters who should study the most—because the lyrics of the songs are what really stick with us. Our understanding matters deeply!

When we meditate on God's Word and truth, we are filling our minds and understanding with God's ways. This is pleasing worship. Just the act of meditating on God's Word is worship, and we need to affirm that truth in the activist age in which we live. I love the way David talks about God's Word in Psalm 19:7–11. After declaring, "The law of the LORD is perfect," he says that the ordinances of God are more precious than gold. There is nothing more valuable than God and His Word. There is nothing more important than meditating on the Word of God and letting it shape our thoughts and our worldview!

During the summer of my engagement (way back when I was eighteen years old), I set myself a goal to memorize Psalm 119 before my wedding day, which was going to happen one week after I turned nineteen, about four months later. I did this to fill my heart and mind with the knowledge that there is nothing more precious than God's Word. It was quite a feeling reciting all 176 verses of Psalm 119 from memory as we drove away from our wedding ceremony in our little red Volkswagen Bug. And when we delight ourselves in God and His Word, He gives us the desire of our hearts!

God's commands are perfect, so when He commands us to love, He is commanding us to do the best thing! There are lots of "Thou shalt not" commands too, but the heart behind them is always the positive "Let Me show you a better way."

And so God invites us to live from our hearts and engage our minds. But true worship never stays there; it must spill over in action.

I want to conclude this chapter with a *once upon a time....* It's a true story, a story of worshipping God in action.

A few years ago I met an amazing man from Ethiopia. His name is Michael Alemu. In 1981, Ethiopia was in a state of revolution. Under the cloak of revolution, the military dictatorship was ordering the killing of many innocent people. Michael was a lieutenant in the army and fought in several battles in eastern and northern Ethiopia at the age of nineteen, witnessing horrendous casualties.

Because his conscience was so devastated over what the army was doing and what was being asked of him, he deserted. His name was put on the most-wanted list as a counterrevolutionary, so he was forced to hide in the jungle. After two months the search intensified, and he knew he must flee his homeland without being able to say good-bye to his family and friends.

After an extremely dangerous six-day journey on foot, he arrived at the Moyale border of Kenya in May 1981 and was escorted like a criminal by the police to Nairobi. On that day, Michael became a refugee. He was one of fifteen thousand given refugee status, status that meant he was stateless (without any rights or access to education or medical help), poor, harassed, and without hope. Here is how Michael described the next six months of his life: "I made the streets, parks, and dark corners of bridges my home. No one seemed to care, and my world was shutting down."

After four months of hopelessness, Michael's life changed on August 15, 1981. God used a seventy-two-year-old man, a bishop in the African Inland Church, to change his life.

Michael was wandering the streets, looking for someone to help him. He decided to go to the African Inland Church head office. It was Saturday morning. He was stopped by a guard who told him that the office was closed and to come back on Monday. As Michael turned away, the guard later said that he felt something inside him stir … he could tell that Michael was in rough shape and that he really needed help. Bishop Ezekiel Breach just so happened to be stopping by his office to do a bit of work and bring home some files. So the guard went against policy and told Michael to slip inside and talk to the bishop, but to make it quick. He opened the large gate and pointed him in the direction of the bishop's office. A few moments later the bishop looked up, surprised to see this filthy man enter his office. He stopped his work and listened to Michael's plea for help. It was eleven in the morning. After hearing Michael's story, the bishop shared the love of God with Michael. As Michael and the bishop prayed together, the Holy Spirit came in what Michael describes as a rush of emotions—in the power of the Holy Spirit, Michael's life was changed!

Michael was filthy, having had no shower or change of clothes in months, but the bishop was not ashamed of him. He embraced Michael and then invited him to take a ride in his nice, clean Volvo. He took him to the best restaurant in town and fed him an amazing meal. He then took him to a hostel, paid the rent for six months, and assigned a pastor to nurture him. The bishop called Michael his special "Saturday, August 15, project." The bishop worshipped in word *and* deed; he took care of his accommodations, food, and clothing. He mentored him and pointed Michael in a meaningful direction for his life. And because Michael had come to faith, he was now linked not only to Bishop Breach but also to the other believers in Nairobi. Through their generosity and encouragement, Michael went to Bible college in that city.

When Michael graduated, Bishop Breach stood by his side as he received a scholarship from the University of Waterloo in Canada, which brought him to Canada ... and eventually brought him into my life.[7] Michael is now married with two beautiful children. He holds two bachelor of arts degrees and a master of social work degree. Today he is serving the Lord through the ministry of Christian Horizons and is currently the VP of Canada/Global Ministries.

We often wonder what difference we can make. The numbers in need overwhelm us. We are not designed to take on the burdens of millions—that's a God-sized job. But we can make a difference in the lives of a few, and for sure all of us can touch one—and when we touch one, the multiplication of the kingdom of God kicks in, for the one who we touch may impact many others.

As Michael describes what he is doing now, think about the fruit of compassion—the guard who played a part by opening the gate, and then a seventy-two-year-old leader in the church, who demonstrated in word and action what it means to be a worshipper of God. Because of the influence of true worshippers, Michael carries on that legacy of true worship today:

> My role is to provide leadership in international development work in Africa, Asia, South America, and North America. I am currently leading programs and projects in twelve countries (including Ethiopia) where we are impacting lives of thousands of marginalized and exceptional people who are in a battle for life. These are the most invisible: children with disabilities who are often treated worse than

animals, their voices never heard, who are hidden
in dark corners of our world. We reach out to them,
share in their pain, and make their fight "the fight
of our generation." We offer disability and children
services, education and training and income proj-
ects, as well as share the Gospel of Jesus Christ
through a holistic ministry.[8]

Pretty awesome, isn't it? And it all started with someone who knew that God was calling him to express his worship through action.

SONGWRITING TIPS

Embrace the AABA song form. The AABA song form is such a wonderful blend of repetition and variation. You come out at the beginning and say the main thing you want to say. Then you say it again (repetition is good!). Then you go to the bridge—an alternate section that provides contrast leading to a climax that longs to resolve back to the A, which you say one more time. This song form keeps a song at a manageable shorter length and helps you focus on the one thing it's all about. It also helps break the pattern of all the verse-chorus songs. Spend some time trying to find some more AABA songs, and get a feel for how they feel different from a verse-chorus song. One of the ways you can tell you are in an AABA song (or any A-based song form) is that the song ends with the A—not the B or the bridge and not the chorus like most verse-chorus songs.

Find fresh ways to express theology and Scripture. When you meditate on Scripture, ask yourself if there is a fresh way to sing it. This song came from my meditation on the greatest command— to love God—and my attempt to paraphrase it. There are so many more passages like this that we need to sing.

Use contrast to awaken people to truth. In this song I state, "There's no higher ground than kneeling down." It doesn't make sense, but then again, it makes complete sense. The word *higher* in contrast with *kneeling down* causes you to really notice both of them, which is the point of contrast.

Be cautious about using the word *worship* or *praise* in your songs. If you need to use one of these words, make sure that it's really warranted by having the rest of the lyric describe in fresh ways what is familiar.

Notes

1. "With All My Affection" by Brian Doerksen © 2002 Integrity's Hosanna! Music/ ASCAP. Used by permission.

2. I'm pretty sure it will be because the descriptions in the book of Revelation describe singing new songs. And just the nature of music itself feels saturated with the character of God.

3. Jesus was living out the words from Deuteronomy 6:5 spoken by Moses. He did not come to speak of a totally new way, but to fulfill, confirm, and complete that which was already revealed.

4. If Abraham had lived after the giving of the Ten Commandments, and a voice had commanded something like this, Abraham would have said, "No, Lord—you said, 'Thou shalt not kill.'"

5. Many scholars and I believe that the site of the crucifixion was Mount Moriah— but it can't be proved.

6. From the song "Thank You for the Cross" as recorded on the Kathryn Scott CD *I Belong.*

7. Michael and I partner together to see special-needs children sponsored and transformed in parts of the world where those with disabilities are considered "cursed by God."

8. You can find more information on the ministry Michael works with at www. chglobal.org.

Song for the Bride (Isaiah 30:15)

I have longed to hold you in My arms
And take all of your fear away
I will take your filthy rags
And make them clean
If you receive My love
If you will receive My love
Return to Me and hear My Spirit say

In repentance and rest
Is your salvation
In quietness and trust
Is your strength[1]

CHAPTER 12

Song for the Bride (Isaiah 30:15)

I'm not going to get into a deep theological debate about gender issues in this book (nor am I qualified to do so!). I just know in my heart that God loves His daughters. The stories of Jesus in the New Testament show Him honoring and lifting up women in a time and place where they were hardly even seen.[2]

But scattered throughout the Scriptures is an image that speaks to what I believe is the core of the feminine heart—the image of a beautiful and pure bride. It's one of the most powerful relational pictures in the Scriptures. The desire to be beautiful, the desire to be the longed-for bride on a perfect wedding day ... this is the picture of how God sees us as His people.

There are two powerful biblical passages that speak of this truth:

> Let us rejoice and be glad and give him glory! For the wedding of the Lamb has come, and his bride has made herself ready. (Rev. 19:7)

> I saw the Holy City, the new Jerusalem, coming down out of
> heaven from God, prepared as a bride beautifully dressed for
> her husband. (Rev. 21:2)

She "[makes] herself ready."

Desire grows.

She is so devoted to her groom that she joyfully submits to a prolonged period of preparation as the yearning in her heart increases for intimacy. The end of that season finally comes … and she is ready, a bride "beautifully dressed for her husband." This picture of preparation is deep within every culture in some form. I believe that God put it there—He wants to use this picture to awaken desire in us, to pull our hearts back to our first love with Him.

In Revelation 19 the multitudes are giving glory to God because the wedding has come and the bride has made herself ready.

The bride's preparation brings glory to God.

The bride's beauty brings glory to God.

There's something amazing about a husband's face and the way other people see him as his beautifully prepared bride approaches him. It never fails to move me. The bride's beauty and preparation bring glory and honor to her husband. And it is faint foreshadowing of the penultimate moment of human history when the beauty of the church, God's people, will be fully revealed.

She will be radiant with beauty.

She will be honored as the most beautiful bride of history.

All of her righteous acts of preparation will be revealed and honored.

And all of her wanderings and unfaithfulness will be forgiven and forgotten. Our Bridegroom will cover us with His glory. He will wipe every tear from our eyes.

Have you ever meditated on the truth that God is your Husband?

This isn't a new idea! Through the prophets and authors of Scripture, God has been revealed as Husband throughout the ages. But we don't seem to like thinking about it (or singing about it) because the intimacy of the image frightens us.

Shortly after I had begun pastoral ministry about twenty years ago, my wife and I attended a seminar in Colorado. A respected prophetic leader got up to speak and told us that God had spoken to him the night before in an audible voice. We all leaned forward—maybe we were expecting something new and spectacular!—and then he spoke these simple, ancient, and powerful words, quoted directly from Isaiah 30:15: "In repentance and rest is your salvation, in quietness and trust is your strength."

I sensed deeply God's presence and confirmation that these are the things God longs for us to experience—and as I meditated on those words being spoken over the church, I realized that He wants the church to return to Him as a bride and allow Him to be our Husband. He longs to be everything we need and love. I felt a stirring to write this Scripture. Sometimes we see worship as a one-way conversation, but I know that God is longing for relationship, so we need to give Him an opportunity to speak into our gatherings as well. One of the ways we can release that is to have some prewritten and spontaneous songs sung from God's heart.

So I set out to write a song based on this Scripture that could be sung over people, with a verse that "set up" Isaiah 30:15 as the chorus. I filled the verse with phrases that spoke of the restoring husband-heart of God—One who is calling out to His beloved who has wandered away. Our return to God always begins with our repentance, a turning back to God and His ways—and ends with resting in God's complete salvation.

Over the centuries God has called to His people through prophets and poets ... and what has the core of the message consistently been?

In one form or another it's been simply this: RETURN TO ME.

I am your Creator ... return to Me!

You have tried to live your life apart from My design, and you are paying the price in your body. Even the whole planet is groaning under the weight of your rebellion against My design. It's time to return to Me, to give Me thanks as your Maker, and to recognize that "the earth is the Lord's, and everything in it."

I am your King ... return to Me!

You have wandered away—out of My realm of authority—and subjected yourself to other rulers and masters, who have turned out to be cruel and heartless. You have lived in the land of fools long enough. It's time to journey back to My land and kingdom and submit yourself to My rule and reign, for I am good, and I long to rule you with kindness and wisdom.

I am your Father ... return to Me!

You have spent your days in orphan living and thinking—trying to create a name for yourself, trying to create your own provision. It's time for you to return to your true family, to be adopted into the real place of belonging and provision. It's time for you to let Me call you by name and to release you into your true identity.

I am your Husband ... return to Me!

Why did you leave Me? What did I do to warrant your rejection? I was always faithful to you; why did you accuse Me of things that are untrue? Why did you blame Me for things I did not do, and why did you wander away from My love? Now you are in a wilderness that is overgrown with weeds, and I long to bring you back into My garden of love. It's time for you to come to your senses and let Me fill you with all the love you have been seeking—I am enough for you.

This is what we hold out as prophets and poets in the congregations and communities where we live. This is what we sing and speak over the nations of the world.

Worship is returning. We were created in God's image to walk with Him in the "cool of the day" (Gen. 3:8) and offer our gratitude and fellowship, but we have wandered away from that relational intimacy.

All too often religion tends to reduce or eliminate the relational realities in Scripture and replace them with religious duty, as if the highest calling we could ever achieve is to learn to do what is right for duty's sake. The Scriptures tell the story of a God with a broken heart—a God who is deeply relational at His core. How else can we even begin to fathom the triune God of grace if not as an eternal relational Being? And so we must turn to some key Scriptures to help shape our understanding of who God is and what drives His pursuit of us. Let's begin with the prophets.

How Do We Know That God Is a Husband?

> "The time is coming," declares the LORD, "when I will make a new covenant with the house of Israel and with the house of Judah. It will not be like the covenant I made with their forefathers when I took them by the hand to lead them out of Egypt, because they broke my covenant, though I was a husband to them," declares the LORD. (Jer. 31:31–32)

> "Return, faithless people," declares the LORD, "for I am your husband." (Jer. 3:14)

The Scriptures clearly state it—and they imply it!

The whole book of Hosea is an illustration of the husband-heart of God for a wayward wife. And think about all the Scriptures that talk about God as a jealous God.

> You shall have no other gods before me.
>
> You shall not make for yourself an idol in the form of anything in heaven above or on the earth beneath or in the waters below. You shall not bow down to them or worship them; for I, the LORD your God, am a jealous God. (Ex. 20:3–5)

The word *jealousy* is part of the vocabulary and language of love. People become jealous when they sense someone else cutting in on a relationship that is exclusively theirs—sounds like a husband and wife, doesn't it?

God's heart is broken when we turn to other loves ... and yet because He created us for love, He must give us the freedom to leave Him. And so He invites ... He calls ... and He waits. And when we are unfaithful, He grieves.

The prophets often used the phrase "prostitute themselves" (see 2 Chron. 21:13); it was God's vivid picture of the extreme unfaithfulness of His people. Why would God use such visceral, offensive imagery?

I believe He uses it because He has a husband-heart, and He longs for a lifelong "forsaking all others" relationship with His people.

By choosing to love one, we are choosing to forsake all others. In our modern culture people don't want to make the choice to forsake all others. People want to play the field relationally and sexually. When we worship God, we are saying that we will willingly choose to forsake all others. When we get married, we are choosing to forsake all others. Love doesn't work unless it's exclusive faithful love.

Listen to part of a traditional wedding vow:

> *Will you have this man to be thy wedded husband, to live together after God's ordinance in the holy estate of matrimony? Will you love him, comfort him, honor him, and keep him in sickness and in health; and, forsaking all others, keep yourself only unto him, so long as you both shall live?*

The phrase "forsaking all others" is foundational to what makes a marriage work.

Here's another part of the traditional wedding vow that couples have exchanged for centuries:

> *With this ring I thee wed, with my body I thee worship, and with all my worldly goods I thee endow.*

What is the source of these vows? Why do they have such power to move us as we hear them exchanged?

Because they are sourced in the divine romance of God with His people.

Listen to the apostle Paul in 2 Corinthians 11:2: "I am jealous for you with a godly jealousy. I promised you to one husband, to Christ, so that I might present you as a pure virgin to him."

God created us as sexual beings, for pleasure and procreation, and He designed it to be one man and one woman for life. Our physical bodies start breaking down with disease when sexual partners are multiplied or when natural sexual relations are exchanged for homosexual relationships. It's simply the way God designed us to function, and no new social or political movement is going to change that.

The intimacy in marriage is rooted in our intimacy with God.

Just as we are created to forsake all others and be devoted to one spouse, we are created to forsake all others and worship one God.

Our worship and devotion belong solely to the one true God revealed in Scripture.

My good friend Steve Mitchinson has written and recorded with Kathyrn Scott one of the most beautiful songs on this theme I have ever heard. The song is called "Divine Romance," and we have used it in worship services—and it also works exquisitely well at weddings!

Divine Romance

I do choose you to be my husband be my lord
To have to hold from this day forward beyond death
So whatever life may bring
Health or sickness, lack or plenty
Receive my offering of faithfulness to you

Forsaking all others living only for you
Forsaking all others living only for you

I do give you my heart and all that I possess
To love to cherish every word and each caress
So whatever life may bring
Joy or sorrow, tears or laughter
Receive this offering of faithfulness to you

Forsaking all others living only for you
Forsaking all others living only for you

As life begins so death completes
Our holy covenant
You take my hand, I'll guide your steps
I'll show you how to dance, this divine romance[3]

Forsaking all others is the *no* that leads to a *yes* of "living only for you." This is what it means to live the life of worship.

We are called to love God, and in order to love God, we need to know who He is. You cannot love someone you don't know. That's why it's so important for us to know the husband-heart of God.

Wouldn't it be tragic if we thought that God was *only* our Master and Judge (which He is as well!), and so lined up our whole lives to serve Him (picturing in our minds the ultimate authority figure like a policeman or judge) and found out as we crossed over to the other side that our Husband was waiting for us, longing for us to love Him? The relationship we have with our local judge or police chief or any authority figure is very different from the relationship between a wife and a loving husband.

It's vital that we know the husband-heart of God because we are called to become like Him—and it's especially vital for us as men, for we are called to "love [our] wives, just as Christ loved the church" (Eph. 5:25). This is our highest calling as men—to be faithful husbands.

Listen to Paul as he writes the church at Ephesus in chapter 5:25–28 (MSG):

> Husbands, go all out in your love for your wives, exactly as Christ did for the church—a love marked by giving, not getting. Christ's love makes the church whole. His words evoke her beauty. Everything he does and says is designed to bring the best out of her, dressing her in dazzling white silk, radiant with holiness. And that is how husbands ought to love their wives. They're really doing themselves a favor—since they're already "one" in marriage.

Go all out in your love for your wives—men, this is quite a calling we have!

We as earthly husbands are to model ourselves after the way that Jesus loves the church.

Here are a few key character traits and actions of a faithful husband seen in Jesus as He relates to the church … and also seen in the best husbands who follow His example.

A Husband Is a Covering

Men are intended by God to provide covering, because this is what God does for us. This is one of the many reasons why the bondage and addiction of pornography is so contrary to the heart of God; instead of covering and protecting women, fallen men are using and exploiting women for their own pleasure and profit.

When a woman leaves her father and mother and becomes united with her husband in marriage, she gets a new identity as she takes his name. Her husband has enfolded her into his name and identity, and it's his calling to be her covering.

God delights in being our covering. Remember that when the Enemy tempts you to hide in your shame. The Enemy exposes people, but God loves to cover us!

A Husband Is Protection

He provides shelter from danger and is physical protection. Women who are alone are much more susceptible to becoming victims of violence and abuse. God as our Husband is our protection.

A Husband Is Provision

A husband's job description is not only to cover and protect; it's also to supply physical needs of shelter, food, and clothing. Most importantly, husbands are called to provide for a wife's emotional needs—letting her know beyond a shadow of a doubt that she is honored and loved.

Over the years of serving in the church and specifically in worship ministry, I have served alongside some single women. I am always careful not to spend time alone with them or foster or encourage an unhealthy bond with them. And I can think of several of these women who have really grasped the truth of the husband-heart of God even though they did not have an earthly husband. And they had to—for who else was going to be their provision and their affirmation?

If you are an adult and single, I pray that you will know the spiritual reality of the Lord as your Husband. Under His covering, protection, and provision, and in the family of God, you can fulfill your calling of extending the kingdom of God in this world.

A Husband Is a Romancer, Initiator, and Pursuer

The last thing I want to say about the qualities of a good husband is one of the most important—and one I see very clearly in the heart of God. It's not good enough for a husband just to provide a safe home and put bread on the table.

A good husband also speaks words of affection, because he

knows what matters to a woman. Many men do this while they are courting, and then after "I do," they don't … but a good husband continues to romance his wife. I often say that dating your spouse is more important *after* the wedding than before. Now that you know so much about each other, will you continue to pursue each other romantically—even when some of the initial feelings have faded? If you do, the reward is a constant renewing of your romantic feelings because you keep investing in your relationship. For Joyce and me this is especially critical, being the parents of some special-needs children, at a staggering risk for divorce. We have done and are doing everything we can to go the opposite way. As I said earlier, we have a weekly date night, and we go away a couple of times a year for a few days or more just to rekindle our romance and our friendship. I turn down many ministry opportunities every year because our marriage cannot sustain too much separation. This is vitally important to me because I see that it is vitally important to God.

Maybe you are saying, "Okay, I can see that an earthly husband like you needs to be a romancer (at least a little bit) … but God? Isn't that taking things too far?"

When I say that God is a romancer, I don't have in mind the sweet, selfish, sentimental concept that is popular in our culture, especially around Valentine's Day.

I use the word "romance" in the biggest, grandest, purest God sense.

God is the one who is drawing us, inviting us, and lavishing us with expressions of love and kindness.

If you want to see the romancing God, simply open your eyes … for the amazing beauty that is all around in creation is a strong testimony that God is a "hopeful romantic." He is trying to woo us to Himself by "sending us bouquets of flowers" and gifts far beyond anything you can purchase with money. The romantic pursuit is in view of a goal; He wants us to accept His proposal of betrothal, saying *yes* to His invitation of love and, then in faithfulness and love, waiting for the great and amazing wedding day, the wedding supper of the Lamb.[4]

God is inviting us as men to be faithful, to be a covering, to be protectors, to be providers, to be romancers and initiators.

What is the Enemy consistently trying to entice men to do?

Not act like God, who is a faithful Husband.

And so I believe our calling as men, for the sake of our wives, daughters, and sons, is to be faithful husbands, and as we "save" our families, that salvation is meant to grow to reach even the women who have been ultimately rejected and used, the prostitutes on the streets of our cities. That's one of my dreams, because I know it's one of God's dreams! I dream that these women who have experienced ultimate rejection would experience the power of redeeming love! I have some friends who work with these women to show them redeeming love, and my wife and I do what we can so that all women can personally know the husband-heart of God.

God invites women into the experience and relationship of worship, and if that worship is saturated with the reality of the husband-heart of God, their broken hearts and lives will be healed. But the Enemy does not want the hearts of women to be healed—he wants to keep the cycle of rejection, shame, and abuse spinning.

I have recently noticed a hunger for *intimacy* all around us— people are reaching for "intimate experiences" … spiritually, sexually, emotionally. Longing for intimacy is a good thing—it is a longing designed and instilled in us by God. The best and truest intimacy is not meant to be just an experience adrift, a fleeting moment with a beautiful stranger. Intimacy is designed to be encased and protected by faithfulness. True intimacy can be experienced only as we forsake all others for the one … and for the One!

We live in a culture and a season of history when people are abandoning their marriage covenants at a crazy rate (sometimes for crazy reasons), often in search of an elusive intimacy, not realizing that the intimacy that they long for is waiting for them in a good marriage—and that ultimate intimacy is waiting for them in biblical worship.

Even in our own churches, people are walking away from marriage believing in a better offer with someone else.

It's important that we lovingly raise a banner of truth. It's important that our messages are filled with the invitation to return.

It's important that our songs of worship are filled with the truth of God as our Husband.

I want to conclude this chapter with a few words for worship leaders. These are not "songwriting tips" so much as convictions of my heart in regard to the work we're called to do. Even if you're not in the role of leading worship, I encourage you to keep reading. What I share will help you pray for those who faithfully strive to lead you to the husband-heart of God.

There is a clear and powerful picture that I never forget as I lead worship. One of the reasons I never forget this picture is because it is attached to great personal loss.

Let me tell you about the story of a friendship that changed my life.

My life was radically changed in the early 1980s when a revival of sorts happened in our little town of Abbotsford, British Columbia. God was moving and stirring up the church—and God was saving people who were far away from Him. I was one of the ones whom God awakened and whom were raised in the church, and Jeff was one of the ones whom God saved out of the world. And God brought us together as best friends. Jeff was actually high on drugs when he had his first Jesus encounter. He came down off drugs and headed to the church building closest to where he lived— it happened to be a Mennonite Brethren church called Bakerview MB. At this time I was part of another local MB church—Central Heights MB—and fairly soon word got out that God was saving some druggies in our town by revealing Himself to them. (We as the church were not doing such a bang-up job on that end, so God took matters into His own hands and simply revealed Himself!) Shortly after Jeff was saved, we met up at a youth revival meeting led by Blayne Greiner and knew immediately that we would be friends for life. We loved serving God together. Often Jeff would speak, and I would lead the music part of the gathering. We were a team. Jeff spent many weekends at our home, and we planned lots of ministry things together. We almost died together one day hiking because we got ourselves into a tight spot on a cliff with no gear! We were both risk takers. And when I told Jeff in 1984 that I was going to be marrying Joyce on November 24 of that year, he committed to helping me prepare. During the weeks leading up to the ceremony, we prayed a lot, talking through details of the day. Then, on that November day in 1984, Jeff and I walked to the front of the church, and instead of the pastor addressing the congregation, Jeff spoke the words of welcome. (I know that's not normal, but Jeff and I were anything but normal in that season of our lives.) He set the stage for what was going to happen ... and then he stepped out of the way and just beamed at us the whole time we were exchanging our vows.

God gave us six more years of friendship until that terrible day on August 6, 1990, when I received the phone call that Jeff had been killed in a tragic hiking accident on a glacier while he was leading a youth camp for his church. In fact, while writing this, I've realized that today is the sixth day of August—the very day the tragedy happened some eighteen years ago.

Shortly after his death I heard someone teach that being a worship leader is like being a best man at a wedding—and I sensed a deep connection to this truth.[5] Jeff had powerfully lived this out in my life, and it was a picture that I would not forget.

In John 3, John the Baptist tries to get people to grasp what motivates him.

> The bride belongs to the bridegroom. The friend who attends
> the bridegroom waits and listens for him, and is full of joy
> when he hears the bridegroom's voice. That joy is mine, and
> it is now complete. He must become greater; I must become
> less. (John 3:29–30)

We as worship leaders are like the friend who attends the bridegroom. We are like the best man at a wedding. The wedding ceremony is not about us—it's about the union of the bride and groom. But we, as the best man, have a role. We help create a setting for the vows to be exchanged. But once the groom and bride are together and exchanging vows … we step out of the way.

This picture has many facets of revelation. And like a metaphor it has limits, too.

Our first job description as "best man" worship leaders is to wait and listen for the Bridegroom's voice. That's where our direction comes from. It doesn't come from what is popular in culture—it comes from knowing Him! Our first and primary calling is to attend the Bridegroom. Our attention is on Him. Our focus is on pleasing Him!

We are never to seek the affection of the bride. Can you imagine the outrage at a wedding ceremony if the best man made a move for the bride? It would be outrageous—but that's what we do as leaders in the church if we place our affections on the church and put too much weight on her opinion of us. Our identity and affection need to come from the Bridegroom!

This can happen from the other side, too… for as the bride waits for the arrival of the Groom, she can become attracted to the best man. This can be hard to resist because there is nothing like the affection of the bride, but our job is to gently but firmly redirect her affection to the Groom.

This is harder to imagine in our culture because we don't have a long period of waiting for the groom. In Jewish culture, after a couple was betrothed, the husband would go away and prepare a home for the bride. The bride was expected to be ready and waiting—for the groom could come at any time to take her away (though it usually took about a year!). In this time of preparation they were considered married. And the groom was not released to go get his bride until his father approved of the home he had prepared for them. (Talk about an amazing parallel between Jewish wedding traditions and the coming return of our Groom, Jesus!)

And so our calling as worship leaders is to encourage the bride while she waits for the Groom—to keep pointing her to Jesus. May the words of John the Baptist become the heart cry of worship leaders everywhere: "He must become greater; I must become less" (John 3:30).

To that end I will continue to pour out my life and my love.

SONGWRITING TIPS

Write some songs from God's perspective. Not every song used in our worship services should be our expression to God. Let Him respond in song and sing over His people. Yes, this is a little scary, but it's vitally important. Let the fear factor drive you to make sure you do your research on these types of songs. You don't want to attribute to God something that He wouldn't say! But don't let fear stop you from taking the risk.

Some of these songs can be spontaneous songs (which some call "the song of the Lord"). I am not a big fan of the term "song of the Lord" because it implies that other songs are not—and these spontaneous songs can be overdone (and overly repetitively simple), but there is still a powerful place for these spontaneous expressions. Ask God to release you to sing His heart over His people! It could be a phrase that just comes into your mind as you are leading worship or a phrase from a Scripture. Make sure you "practice" this in private and small groups before you do it with a large group!

Sing the words of Scripture. There is something so powerful and timelessly right about singing Scripture over people. It carries an authority that is far beyond our creative words.

Use chordal movements to create tension and release. I start this song on the V (five) minor, and this brings in immediate tension with darker colors present. From there I move to the I (one) chord and resolve the tension. This matches the words "I have longed to hold you"—the tension speaks of the separate and subsequent longing, and the coming home to the I (one) chord speaks of the "in My arms." The chords and their movement are saying the same thing as the lyrics. Make sure the songs you write present a good match between the tension and release of your chords and the lyrical message of the song.

Notes

1. Brian Doerksen, "Song for the Bride (Isaiah 30:15)," © 1990 Vineyard Songs Canada and ION Publishing. Used by permission.

2. Christianity's supposed suppression of women and their rights has nothing to do with God and His heart and everything to do with humanity's fallenness and desire to stay in control! Christianity and Jesus are the greatest champions of women in history!

3. Steve Mitchinson, "Divine Romance," © 2007 ION Publishing. Used by permission.

4. At our wedding day on November 24, 1984, Joyce and I had a banner behind the head table at our reception: "Blessed are those who are invited to the wedding supper of the Lamb."

5. I believe the teacher was David Boyd, a worship leader from Colorado.

NEW FROM **BRIAN DOERKSEN**

IT'S TIME

FRESH NEW RECORDINGS... PASSIONATE GUITAR DRIVEN WORSHIP

INCLUDING...
It's Time For The Reign Of God
Come Now Is The Time To Worship
Refiner's Fire
Hallelujah (Your Love Is Amazing)
Holy God
Hope Of The Nations
Come And Fill Me Up
...and many more

Available at your favorite
Christian bookstore, iTUNES or
www.integritymusic.com